On Board with Bradley

On Board with Bradley

THE COLLECTED COLUMNS FROM
MOTOR BOATING & SAILING MAGAZINE,
1977 to 1983

by Dick Bradley

Introduction by Vicki Carkhuff

Illustrations by James E. Mitchell

MOTOR BOATING
& SAILING

Hearst Marine Books / New York 1983

Library of Congress Catalog Card Number: 83-81219

ISBN: 0-688-02483-1

Printed in the United States of America

First Edition

1 2 3 4 5 6 7 8 9 10

BOOK DESIGN BY LINEY LI

Contents

On Board with Bradley

Introduction

For a year and a half, our trawler lay next to the Bradleys' yacht, *Simba*, on the New River in Fort Lauderdale. When Dory and I reminisce about those days, we remember them as being almost idyllic. Our two boats, along with seven others, were tied behind a quiet hotel in the heart of town. There were showers, a pool, a lawn, a grocery store, a post office all close by. Best of all, *Simba* lay next to the coolest tree in all Fort Lauderdale, a wide fanning fig beneath which the three of us ate lunch nearly every day.

I remember those lunches with great affection. Dick Bradley was always a great talker—I used to kid him that for $300, he would argue either side of any question. Some days our discussion got to the point where Dory would get up and start varnishing. But on other days, Bradley would verbally lead us along a path that meandered through his life: his childhood in Chicago spent playing tennis and hooky (my favorite story from that era was the day his history teacher called his mother to say that her son had to be a genius—there was no other conceivable explanation for the fact that he was receiving a grade of 45 in her class while doing absolutely no work); his growing up to become an adman with various agencies in Chicago; his marriage to Dory, who paid for his divorce from his first wife; their early days in La Jolla; their introduction to boating with a small powerboat and then later the Eight-Meter *Cheerio;* their balmy days at the San Diego Yacht Club, where they won the Ensenada Race in 1962 and Bradley founded (much to the dismay of the legitimate users of San Diego Harbor) the Wednesday Night Beer Can Series; the rearing of their two daughters, Linda and Barbara; their move east and the series of sail- and powerboats they owned and cruised along the east coast; the acquisition of *Simba,* their fifty-two-foot Huckins; Bradley's debut as a monthly columnist for *Motor Boating and Sailing;* his duels in the column with such overfatted calves as the feminist movement and Howard Ruff; and his brief career as a yacht broker. Over the course of that year and a half, from lunch to lunch, Bradley had a hundred good ideas for increasing his kitty, allowing the two of them to continue their maximum life-style by minimum means. For a brief time he also had a career as the publisher of a yachting magazine called *Helm*—which never got to the newsstands—but another project did come to fruition—two canal trips through France.

One of the many projects that Bradley toyed with during that time was the publication of a collection of his columns and letters. He talked endlessly to publishers and printers, designers of covers, and typesetters. And these discussions went on and on until it became clear to Dory and me that Bradley was stalling. The inescapable conclusion was that although he was bluff and bold and self-confident on the exterior, when it got right down to it, he was afraid of what the reaction to the book would be. In the end, he made the ultimate procrastination.

Bradley, the man, was exactly the one we all see in these columns—he hated hard work but was absolutely tireless in stirring up controversy and devilment. (The night he mooned the *Jungle Queen* was one of his most notorious stunts.) He had no patience for anything he considered boring but lots of time to plot sticking the old Bradley needle into anyone's overinflated balloon. He was slow to pick up a dinner tab but always quick to help any of his troops of friends. He loved all things to do with boats—in coastal waters, that is—a good discussion, good food, and above all, Dory.

It's too late now for all of us to tell Bradley that we loved his book. It'll never be too late, though, thank goodness, to sample Bradley's cockeyed view of the world, to enjoy his wit, and to remember the man.

—VICKI CARKHUFF

ONE

Unable-Bodied Seaman

An Anchor to Leeward

⚓ *NOVEMBER, 1977*

The West Palm Beach Cruisin', Boozin' and Snoozin' Club was having its regular Wednesday Yachtsman's Lunch, which meets on Thursdays to thwart moochers and women's libbers.

The lunch dishes had been cleared away, everybody's glasses had been refilled for the fourth time and the Commodore called the meeting to order by pounding the table with a beer bottle.

"Does anybody have a sea story to tell us?" he inquired.

An elderly gentleman arose and walked slowly to the microphone.

"Gentlemen," he said, to an enthusiastic round of applause, "I have a story to tell you about that wonderful old couple we all know and love, Cedric and Sibyl Hitchcock. Through their books and magazine articles we have been able to follow their progress as they circumnavigate the globe every two years in their vessel, *Voyager X* or *XI* or whatever.

"Few of us ever have the opportunity to witness this gallant pair in action. I am fortunate to have just returned from the Bahamas

"The Hitchcocks are coming! The Hitchcocks are coming!
It's every man for himself!"

where I watched a performance seldom equaled in the annals of sailing. Let me set the scene for you. It was a typical April day at Stocking Island in the Exumas. Above was the brilliant blue sky with an occasional puffy white cloud. All around the anchorage, skippers and crews were enjoying after-lunch siestas.

"Suddenly, the silence was broken by loud cheers. I looked up to see signal flags being hoisted as though to welcome a person of great importance. I flagged down a passing skiff and asked what was causing all of the excitement.

" 'The Hitchcocks are coming! The Hitchcocks are coming! It's every man for himself!' With this warning the skiff sped away to alert other skippers who might not be familiar with the Hitchcock Method of Anchoring. A combination of faulty eyesight and an unreliable reverse gear have resulted in mishaps in nearly every cruising harbor around the globe. Luckily, we had ample time to prepare for their arrival.

My wife came up from the engine room where she had been changing the oil and asked, 'What shall we do? Our insurance expired two years ago and I know Cedric won't pop for repairs.'

"I had been surveying the situation and felt certain *Voyager X* or *XI* or whatever wouldn't be able to reach us. We were situated behind a shoal that had only four feet of water at low tide. *Voyager X* or *XI* or whatever draws nearly nine feet, even though it is only thirty-two feet overall.

"Don't worry, my dear. There is no way old Cedric can get to us. I predict he'll fetch up on yonder shallow spot. Cedric has a penchant for sand bars.

"Gentlemen, the scene reminded me of Dunkirk. Every pair of eyes was fixed on the horizon. Some younger crew members had placed themselves in the spreaders of their boat, whether to be first to cry, 'Sail ho' or in hopes of avoiding injury, I cannot say.

"Just before sunset a cry went up, 'Here they come! Here comes *Voyager X* or *XI* or whatever.'

"At this, fenders were hung over the sides, mattresses were positioned to provide maximum protection and everyone was armed with boat hooks for fending the stalwart little ship off.

"Soon she could be seen, tacking against a stiff wind, with Cedric at the wheel and Sibyl manning the genoa sheets and the running backstays. A remarkable performance for a ninety-year-old woman with a bad back. Cedric could be seen peering into the mist through his rheumy eyes. Unfortunately, Cedric is in a mist even on the clearest of days.

"They sailed up to the mouth of the cove under full sail and at hull speed, estimated at four knots. Suddenly, Sibyl looked up from grinding on the genoa winch and realized they were entering the cove. In a flash she had let the genoa fly, dropped the main (and the boom on Cedric's head, Sibyl having forgotten to take up on the topping lift), and ran to the bow, arms flapping wildly as she screamed at Cedric in her quavering voice, 'Back down, fall off, start the engine . . . do something!'

"But crusty old Cedric was not one to panic. 'Not to worry, my pet,' he called out in a calm voice. 'Just be ready to drop the anchor when I give you the signal.'

"Sibyl, ever dutiful wife and crew member that she is, picked up the ninety-pound plow anchor in her arms and climbed out on the long bowsprit, ready to let the anchor go when given the order. But, just as I predicted, *Voyager X* or *XI* or whatever came a cropper on the sand bar and Sibyl did a glorious jackknife, entering the water with a minimum of splash considering she was holding the anchor, and disappeared.

"Well, gentlemen, you can imagine the applause old Cedric received at this remarkable performance. It was a sight I shall never forget. There was *Voyager X* or *XI* or whatever with her nose deep in the sand, her stern high out of the water, her genoa flapping madly, her main covering the cockpit and old Cedric standing on the rail, bowing graciously and accepting the plaudits of the crowd with the poise of a true entertainer and sportsman.

"Within moments everyone in the anchorage had accepted his invitation to come aboard and inspect the famous yacht. Knowing that Cedric wouldn't have booze or ice or crackers aboard, each guest brought his own bottle and snacks. Well, gentlemen, I can assure you it was one hell of a great party. One magazine writer asked Cedric to describe his anchoring technique and mentioned how gracefully Sibyl had flown through the air as she dove the anchor.

"A look of horror crossed the writer's face as he realized that Sibyl was still in the water. A great cry went up and all aboard rushed to the rail.

"'Not to worry, my friends. Sibyl is an excellent swimmer,' Cedric assured us. And perhaps she had been, some forty years before.

"Gentlemen," our elderly raconteur concluded, "we may have seen the last of Sibyl, but Cedric is still with us. In fact, while we have been enjoying our lunch, *Voyager X* or *XI* or whatever sailed into our marina under full canvas and, unless I'm mistaken, is sharing a slip with Doctor Swanson's seventy-two-foot Trumpy. I hope you're insured, Doctor, as his bow appears to be imbedded in your transom."

For those of you who have not met Cedric, I give you this warning. Keep a sharp lookout for an ancient cutter with a rumpled bow and a skipper with failing eyesight and an unreliable reverse gear. Without Sibyl, his landings are more spectacular than ever.

Watts New in Faro Blanco

⚓ *APRIL, 1982*

I'm not one who goes in for a lot of electronic gadgetry. Not that I don't find it fascinating, because I do, but because I can't afford to buy most of the goodies available.

That's why I am not turned on by such instruments as an electronic anchor-dragging alarm. My solution has always been to attach a cluster of empty beer cans to a sash weight by a light line. I put the cans on the cabin top above where we sleep and drop the sash weight directly off the bow of the boat. If the boat swings or drags during the night, the cans come crashing down on the deck and I'm awake in two seconds. It's not a very sophisticated system, but it works like a charm.

My electronic equipment is pretty basic. I also have an aging flasher depth sounder and an ancient recording depth sounder that Bendix probably stopped making twenty-five years ago. I have an AM and marine channel receiver with a huge loop that revolves. They all work just fine. I almost threw it overboard a couple of years ago on the advice of an electronic salesman, only to find that the reason it wasn't working was because the speaker wire had come loose. I have an old-fashioned intercom and loud hailer that has expired totally, so I just raise my voice level a few decibels. My autopilot, original equipment some thirty years ago, gave up the ghost and I said, "To hell with it. I'll just steer the boat myself."

I have no need for Sat-Nav or Loran because I know where I am 99 percent of the time. A Sat-Nav would merely affirm the fact that *Simba* is securely tied to the dock at Faro Blanco in the Florida Keys and will, in all likelihood, remain in that beautiful spot for the foreseeable future. We'll be in Europe most of the summer and no Florida boat owner would be caught dead cruising in the winter months. Should we decide to take our boat to New England, I might be tempted to buy a radar. In fact, I swore I would never again cruise in New England without radar. And inasmuch as a trip up the waterway to Newport, Rhode Island, seldom takes me out of sight of land, I have just about all the electronic gear I need.

Wait a minute! I forgot to mention the only new item I've bought in the last six years. It may be the best investment I've ever made in electronics. My tired, obsolete radiotelephone stopped functioning about a year ago. It was an awful piece of junk, even at its best. Dory refused to let me take the boat out of the slip without a radio and whatever Dory says goes aboard this vessel. I did some investigating and found that the successful fishermen in this fishing paradise were sold on a set that allowed them to determine the direction from which the signal was coming. In other words, if they overheard two fishermen talking about where the big ones were biting, the set told them where the lucky fisherman was located. All they had to do was head off in that direction and snuggle up next to his anchorage. Now, that was my idea of fishing, and my idea of a proper radio, as well.

As is customary when making a major investment, I consulted with Dory. This is necessary because Dory won't let me sign checks or carry more than five dollars in cash in my billfold. (I'm supporting equal rights all the way in hopes of achieving a better status on the boat.) I explained that the set I wanted was about three times as expensive as a cheap set, but pointed out that we could home in on where the Coast Guard was located when trying to find our way to Block Island in a dense fog. I then described how this particular set would lead me directly to where the fish were biting.

"Don't bother to tell me about the fishing advantages. You won't catch any more fish with this super gadget than you did without it. What interests me is that bit about being able to find our way to Block Island in the fog. Are you sure this thing really works?" she asked.

"Look, I've talked with ten commercial fishermen and they say they couldn't survive without it. Then I talked with the local dealer and he said he's selling lots of them," I assured her.

"Okay," she said. "But it's your Christmas present and don't start sniffling if you don't find anything else in your stocking on Christmas morning."

Now I have what is undoubtedly the finest piece of electronic gear I've ever owned. It's called a Regency Polaris NC7200. It has this little scanner with a light that revolves until somebody comes on any channel I want to monitor. Then it stops and points out the direction that signal is coming from. It has four weather channels (I can listen to Key West's weather and Miami's weather and decide which way to head for sunshine). Not only that, it has three separate computer controlled memories to make up for my own failing non-computerized memory. I love it! Sometimes, when TV is even worse than usual, I just sit and watch the little light go round and round, listening to fishermen lie about how many fish they're catching or to confused skippers trying to describe their general location to the Coast Guard. There's a certain feeling of power in knowing where people are when they don't know that you know.

Has it improved my fishing? Not yet. Nor has it helped me find a harbor in the fog. This isn't the fault of the Regency Polaris, understand. It's working just great. The problem lies in my starboard engine's reverse gear. It won't reverse. Or go into forward, either, for that matter. And to think that those damned engines were brand new just thirty years ago!

But as soon as the reverse gear is fixed and I save up enough money to buy fuel, I'm heading out into the wild blue water, with one ear tuned to the Polaris and one eye on the little revolving light. Then let those tuna and grouper and sailfish look out. I'm about twenty years overdue for a real strike.

Meantime, should you be lost in the area of Marathon in the Keys, just holler for help. I'll hear you and I'll know just where you are. If you're lost I can tell you where you are in relation to where I am. But then you're on your own. To me you'll just have to remain a little orange blip on a scanner. Sorry about that, pal.

Unable-Bodied Seaman

⚓ *JULY, 1978*

My answer to seamanship is to avoid getting into situations which call for it. During the twenty-five years I've been sailing or powering around, the only serious problems I've faced were the result of stupidity, bad luck, lethargy, negligence, or two martinis before lunch. Seamanship has never influenced either the accident or the solution.

For example, last winter I was securely anchored in a hurricane-proof harbor on Man-O'-War Cay in the Abacos. The only real danger there under normal circumstances is collision with a bareboat charterer, so when I retired one night with bottle fatigue after a memorable on-shore party, I had only one concern: whether to take two aspirins immediately or four the next morning. I don't remember my decision.

What I do remember is Dory, my wife, nudging me at 4:30 A.M. and asking if I heard a bell ringing. There were certainly some bells, not to mention sirens and buzzing sounds, going off in my much-abused head, but gradually the realization set in that somewhere on the boat, a strange bell *was* ringing. I got out of bed and traced the bell to a cabinet, found the switch, and cut off the sound in hopes that I was dealing with a faulty switch or wiring connection. This mood of optimism lasted until I walked aft to the galley and realized I was standing in a foot of water.

"Dory!" I yelled. "Get up!"

"What is it?" she asked.

"We're sinking!" I replied.

Then I lifted the cockpit hatch and discovered the watertight engine compartment was three feet in water, with streams of seawater pouring through holes in the canvas boots which surrounded the inboard ends of my through-transom rudder levers. It was obvious that my bilge pumps couldn't cope. The only answer seemed to be to get a heavy-duty pump off another boat in the anchorage. I decided that the fifty-foot trawler *Buster,* owned by two experienced sailing types, Bill and Dorothy Hopkins, was the most likely source.

I vaguely recall at that point putting out a Mayday on the VHF, starting both engines, flashing a spotlight at *Buster,* and shooting off rapid-fire instructions (most of which were countermanded a moment later) to Dory. With tears streaming down her face, she took over the VHF, got me into a pair of pants, flashed the spotlight around and made herself useful while I wrung my hands, stared at the rising water and wondered how I could explain *this* one to my long-suffering insurance agent.

It finally became obvious to me that the only solution was to run the boat up on a shoal, which would prevent her from sinking in fifteen feet of water. By this time, the wind had picked up to 45 knots, and the problem was how to get free of the two anchor lines that were splayed out Bahamian style. I asked (ordered, she says) my wife to get a knife and cut the anchor lines. As she cut one, I threw off another, and we promptly hit an anchored old hulk, but a hole in the bow seemed minor at this point.

Finally, with both lines free, I started to maneuver through the anchored boats and onto the shoal at the harbor entrance. At this critical moment, the starboard engine died. (We had wrapped one of our anchor lines around both props, causing one to stall out, we discovered later.) With one engine gone, no maneuvering room and 45 knots of wind, the situation was nip and tuck. Even the lights going on aboard *Buster* couldn't eradicate the hard fact that I was drifting down on a thirty-five-foot sloop which lay between us and a dock. The skipper had been awakened by the roar of my engines and, as we closed on him, he roused his family to fend off before his eleven-foot beam was reduced to eight and a quarter. He quickly threw off his anchor lines and managed to squeeze out behind us, just as we crunched up against the dock.

So there we were, at a dock but sinking in the deepest part of the harbor, when our friend from the *Buster* showed up in his dinghy. Taking one look at our predicament, he went back to his boat, pulled a Pacer gasoline-powered pump out from beneath his wife's bunk and came back as fast as his little one-cylinder engine could push him. The Pacer went onto the coaming, one hose dropped into the bilge, Bill gave it a tug and, presto, a two-inch stream of water shot out of the other end. Within a few minutes we were pumped dry in both the engine room and the galley compartment. About five minutes later Marcel Albury showed up with one of his ferry boats and towed us to a dock where we borrowed a heavy-duty sump pump and kept it handy just in case.

To my knowledge, there are no books covering such situations, and yet I'm told a lot of boats do sink at their moorings or in a slip for a variety of reasons. In my case, a haul-out and inspection revealed the cause of the accident to be a small fracture in the glass-sheathed wood bottom just above my starboard propeller. My propellers had picked up a wood block or similar projectile and hurled it against the bottom of the boat while anchoring. Water seeped in during the night, causing the boat to settle to the point where the rudder levers were below the waterline. The rudder boots, having developed a few weak spots, burst under pressure and in came the sea, gallons and gallons of it.

True, I was lax in allowing my rudder boots to get rotten, lazy for not diving over and inspecting the hull when I first heard a thump as I maneuvered to anchor that afternoon, cheap for not having installed automatic switches on my bilge pumps, shortsighted for not having a Pacer pump, untidy for not vacuuming the bilges for debris that could clog the limber holes, and lacking in foresight for not knowing that someday all these errors of omission would combine to cause me a near heart attack.

"Poor seamanship," I can hear some of you old salts saying. Maybe so, but my boat did not sink and it is in better shape now than it was before. Even if my crew had consisted of Hal Roth, Jerry Cartwright and Eric Hiscock, the end result would have been the same. Without Bill Hopkins and his magic pump, we'd all have ended up swimming ashore.

Seamanship makes great reading, but it's pretty hard to remember the rules when you're up to your knees in water, the wind is blowing a gale, your props are wound up in your anchor line and your wife is standing on the bow of your boat waving boats out of your way with, "Look out! We're coming through!"

To me, seamanship is doing whatever has to be done to stay afloat and that generally means using your head, staying calm and having a buddy nearby with a big, powerful pump.

Inflate to Live

⚓ *SEPTEMBER, 1981*

A friend once asked me to recommend the best value in boating, in my not so humble opinion. My answer was quick and enthusiastic. The most fun I've ever had, per dollar invested, was an inflatable runabout of ancient vintage that had spent most of its years banging around the Caribbean aboard that beautiful ketch, *Ticonderoga.*

By the time I bought it from then-owner Ken McKenzie in the fall of 1977, that tired old Zodiac had survived countless beachings, batterings, hurricanes, and could rightly have been relegated to patch material. I'd seen McKenzie inflating his new runabout on the docks in Newport, Rhode Island, and figured he'd be anxious to unload the old one on some unsuspecting soul. I even harbored the unlikely dream that he might give me the old girl just because of our friendship. Fat chance!

When I finally sidled up to him and asked if he'd thrown away his old Zodiac yet, he allowed that he did have a mint-condition pre-owned model that he might let go at a bargain price for a good buddy. The "bargain price" he mentioned was slightly less than brand new at full retail and I politely declined, reminding him that I was old enough to recognize a waterfront horse trader when I saw one.

He was due to leave for the islands in a few days, and I let him stew overnight. The next day he approached me with a big smile, wondering when I wanted to pick up my new mini-yacht. I told him I couldn't afford his price and he lowered it a wee bit. I countered with an offer of fifty dollars in cash and twenty-six cases of Stroh's beer I had acquired through a bit of chicanery that summer. When he re-fused with a rather insulting remark, I went back to my hard-to-get posture. Another day passed and Ken dropped his price again. This time I asked where I might view his precious bit of nautical memora-bilia and was assured it was stored away in a safe, dry place. Under

... And away I'd go at top speed.
What a romantic picture I must have made.

thousands of pounds of old sail bags and miscellaneous junk, I finally uncovered what appeared to be a halfway house for wayward rodents. My dear wife, who was against the deal from the beginning, said, "It looks like it was used to evacuate the British Army at Dunkirk. If you pay over ten dollars for that relic, you're out of your mind."

I waited until McKenzie was untying his dock lines and said, "I'll give you a hundred dollars and twelve cases of Strohs."

"Make it one hundred fifty dollars cash," he whined. "But I'm losing my butt on the deal."

I rushed back to the boat, found the checkbook which Dory had squirreled away, and huffed back to *Ti* just as she cast off. I handed him the check and he hollered, "I hope this check doesn't bounce."

I answered in kind, "Your dumb inflatable better inflate *and* float!"

I have to admit it was the most disreputable piece of equipment I have ever owned. It was scarred and patched and bedraggled. The first time I unrolled it, a crowd gathered and betting commenced. I just went ahead inserting the floorboards while Dory pumped and griped (she's multitalented in some areas) and soon found myself the proud owner of a seemingly sound, if not beautiful, runabout. There was one minor problem: a faint hissing sound. As it turned out, an old patch had given way. With a dab of glue here and a bit of pressure there the hissing stopped, the applause began, and I was ready to go mini-yachting.

With a shiny new Evinrude 15 h.p. on the stern, an extension handle on the throttle and hundreds of square miles of Bahamian water to play in, I became known as the Madman of Man-O'-War. Four or five times a day I would jump into my Zodiac, grab the painter in my left hand, the handle in my right, and away I'd go at top speed, racing through the anchorage. What a romantic picture I must have made. Skinny legs supporting a pot belly, gray beard and long hair streaming in the wind, teeth clamped to avoid swallowing no-see-ums and bifocals covered with salt, scaring the hell out of innocent yachties rowing ashore in their eight-foot dinghies. I was a wrinkled, slightly senile child with his new toy. I loved it!

On Sundays we would hop into the Zodiac and zip over to the Harbor Lodge in Hope Town for brunch. Weekdays we would run to Marsh Harbor to shop or have lunch at Wally Smith's fabulous Conch Inn. Occasionally, I would take Old Zody out for a day of fishing. And every late afternoon we could be found making our way from boat to boat in American Harbor, cadging drinks from newcomers. On those occasions when Dory would say, "I want to get some cleaning done and I don't want you underfoot," I'd putt-putt slowly around the island, sulking a bit but relishing the clear water. I recall with particular pleasure one late afternoon when I drifted over a shoal area in a very light breeze, staring at the bottom just inches below and resisting the temptation to touch the variety of sea life within reach of my fingers. I recall thinking that I would never, never return to the insanity of urban sprawls like Fort Lauderdale and that I would keep Old Zody until she was ready to be ensconced in the Inflatable Hall of Fame . . . or the Smithsonian.

But even the best laid plans go astray and I recently woke up to discover that I had spent three whole years of my life bouncing around on the New River in Fort Lauderdale. "Enough is enough," I cried. "I want to go somewhere where I can tie Old Zody alongside. I want to go where I can zoom over clear green water without being run over by a moron in a sixty-foot macho boat screaming down the waterway at fifty miles per hour. I want to go where the . . ."

As frequently happens, just when I am waxing poetic, Dory puts her few cents in and spoils the mood. "Knock it off, Bradley. You gave that speech a month ago. We *are* moving where the water is green, remember? And when you get to Faro Blanco you have my permission to make a perfect ass of yourself, if that's what makes you happy. But I've got news for you. Old Zody has new owners."

"That's ridiculous," I said. "I'll never part with my faithful ship, even though she has seen better years. By the way, who are the new owners?"

"I gave it to Linda and Chelsea. I knew you wouldn't mind my giving it to your own daughter and granddaughter. You're mean, but not that mean. And besides, you only paid a hundred fifty dollars for it."

"That's not the point," I protested. "What will I use to visit all the new friends we are going to make down in the Keys? Where will I go when you throw me off the boat?"

"I've got a little surprise for you," Dory said, with a sneaky smirk on her pretty face.

"You've already given me one surprise and I didn't like it."

"A-h-h, but this you're going to like," she said. "I've ordered a brand-new inflatable called a Grand Raid. It's bigger and roomier and safer and faster than Old Zody. Besides, she's gorgeous. I put money down on it last week and all you have to do is make the payments."

"Good Lord, woman, I can hardly pay for what we already have, much less a new Zodiac."

"All it takes is increased production on your part. If you start typing right now and keep it up you'll have that new toy paid for in no time. You've got thirty days before the first payment comes due."

With a wife like Dory, I'll be in deep trouble if I ever develop arthritis in my fingers. Meantime, if you don't see me on the dock for a while, you'll know why. I'll be typing as fast as I can.

Break Boating's Filthiest Habit

⚓ *MAY, 1979*

Show me a clean engine room, and I'll show you a skipper who never changes his own oil!

Oh, changing oil sounds simple: All it requires is the ability to pump oil out of the engines into empty containers and then refill the engines with clean oil. Simple enough on the face of it. But I offer myself as living proof that oil changing is beyond the capability of the average fumble-fingered boat owner. For the past twenty-five years, I've looked on engine rooms as Black Holes of Calcutta where no sane man ventures except under duress.

Frankly, I ask not what I can do for my engines, but only what my engines can do for me. It's enough that they clank away in seeming contentment until we reach our landfall. But every time I turn around, some guy on TV is warning me to "see him now or see him later," implying that failure to do so will require a new pair of engines, a fate worse than death, or both.

So, like millions of other naïve engine owners, I dutifully descend into the bowels of the ship armed with cans, pumps, hoses, rags, drop cloths, overalls, wrenches, and the sure knowledge that disaster will befall me before the job is completed.

Why don't I just run my boat into a yard and say "Do me," the way my wife, Dory, does with Elizabeth Arden? For one thing, "doing" a pair of GM 6-71s means replacing some sixty-four quarts of black gook at a dollar fifty a quart, plus paying eighteen dollars an hour for a petroleum transfer engineer to do the job. There aren't any five-dollar-an-hour mechanics anymore. They're an extinct species, like garbagemen, janitors, and other highly skilled nudnicks.

As a result of an extended case of poverty, I've been changing my own oil for many years. Unfortunately, this is a situation where practice does not make perfect. I inevitably end up with containers overflowing, hoses whipping around like angry cobras spouting black venom, gaskets failing to seat properly, and an engine bilge full of oil that takes at least three weeks of constant scrubbing and pumping to pass inspection. Try as I will, I still end up leaving a trail of oily footprints on the decks and the carpets. And whatever areas I miss are filled in by our inquisitive kitten. The only benefit of all this is that the boat is filled with an icy silence for several days, and in Florida in mid-summer, this is a welcome relief.

But all of that is now behind me. I have seen the light and it comes in the form of a piece of equipment that looks like a chrome-plated paint can. You have it hooked up to your engine and you never change oil again! You heard me. You never change oil again. What happens is beyond my ability to describe. All I know is that these gadgets continually clean, refine, and purify your oil while your engine is running, and it stays as pure as the driven snow forever and ever. Oh, what a relief it is!

I'm hesitant to tell you the name of this wonder-working contrivance because I know I'll get a lot of flak, but here goes. The thing is called a Purifiner because it purifies and refines your oil on a continuing basis. You can now ask yourselves what in hell Dick Bradley would know about purity or refinement and you can keep the answer to yourself. Purifiners were brought to my attention by Dick Bertram when he mentioned having found a system for avoiding oil changing while preparing a yacht for cruising in Europe. He didn't mention the name so it took me a while to locate the source, which turned out to be right here in Florida.

Normally, I'd have passed off the company's claims as pure hype. I've been a cynic since the time I discovered the truth about Santa Claus, the tooth fairy, and the stork, not necessarily in that order. Why hadn't I heard about Purifiners before? After all, they'd been on the market for a couple of years, during which the bureaucrats were moaning about oil shortages. Yet here was a system for using oil forever, simply by keeping it clean and free of water, fuel, acids, and all sorts of junk. Why had it been kept a secret? Could it be that the major oil companies didn't want us to know about Purifiners? No, that couldn't be. That would be un-American.

But now the secret is out. The truth is that oil does not break down mechanically. Government sources will admit that. What happens is that oil becomes unusable when it is dirty. Keep it clean and it lasts forever. Engine builders like GM, Cummins, Caterpillar, and all the others assure owners that using Purifiners will not affect their warranties. When you install them on your engines you don't even put in new oil. These things will bring your dirty oil back to clean condition while you're running.

But what about those warnings to change oil or else? Well, I can remember my mother telling me that I should eat everything on my plate because millions of people were starving in China. So now I'm fifty pounds overweight, and I'm so accustomed to saving the lives of starving Chinese that I can't appear in public in swim trunks. And what about the new oil one company claims can go for twenty-five thousand miles in a car without changing? Sure it can, providing you have a Purifiner in your car. Otherwise, you're going to have an engine full of filthy oil, and that shouldn't happen to any decent, hard-working engine.

One of the country's biggest moving-van lines just bought eleven thousand Purifiners for their trucks. The U.S. Navy thinks it's now solved the oil-changing problem for submarines. But all of that is peanuts to what it means to cruising yachtsmen. It means freedom from hours of torture hanging upside down, batlike, in a cramped engine room. Freedom from watching some yo-yo charge you eighteen hard-earned bucks an hour to do what you could do if you weren't so damned clumsy.

I can hardly wait for some mechanic to pull out the dipstick in my engine, shake his head and then, with a concerned expression on his face, say, "I'd better change your oil, mister. It really is dirty."

I've rehearsed my answer. It is short, succinct, and to the point. "Buzz off!"

The Fine Points of Anchoring

⚓ *AUGUST, 1978*

The way I see it, if God had meant for man to anchor, He would have made all harbors a uniform twelve-feet deep with firm, sandy bottoms, no adverse currents or sudden wind shifts, no hidden underwater snares such as cables, pieces of chain, old anchors, rocks, tree stumps or grassy patches. But, as any of you who have anchored can testify, there's no doubt in anyone's mind exactly where God stands on this particular subject.

I came to this conclusion a few months back when I was sprawled in my cockpit, guzzling a soothing drink and recuperating from one of my more traumatic anchoring efforts. My hands shook, my shirt was soaked with perspiration, my voice was hoarse from shouting orders to my wife, and my nervous system seemed to consist of millions of exposed wires that had shorted out somewhere along the line. I can't explain it, but anchoring in a strange harbor does me in, even when that harbor is as nearly perfect as Man-O'-War's American Harbor in the Abacos.

Negotiating the shallow, narrow and rock-lined cut into Man-O'-War had put me into a somewhat apprehensive state of mind, but it wasn't until I got my first glimpse of the fleet anchored inside that I broke out in a cold sweat. Gathered there was as critical an audience as any anchorer could face. Skippers and crew of every boat in the harbor had come on deck to watch the latest clown make a fool of himself. In the absence of television, watching boats anchor becomes the main entertainment with cruising people.

I hadn't expected to be performing for such a large turnout, so I had neglected to take my Valium. My mouth was dry and my heart was beating faster than normal as I did what every skipper does in this situation. I assumed a rather bored expression, slouched nonchalantly behind the wheel with a beer in one hand and the wheel in the other, and worked my way through the fleet, silently praying that somewhere, somehow there was a place for me to drop my hook.

Being mid-afternoon, most of the choice locations had been taken, which meant that no matter where I anchored someone would feel I was too close. Had I been maneuvering a sailboat with a tiny engine murmuring away, I might have slipped into a good spot and had the anchors down before I was noticed. But with two big 6-71s roaring away, my old dog relieving herself on the foredeck, and my wife and I communicating at the tops of our voices, I knew my every move was being analyzed and criticized by the entire fleet.

Each time I thought I'd found a likely location, the skippers on the nearest boats would walk to their foredecks and give me long, searching looks that said quite clearly, "Not here, stinkpotter!" But finally I'd reached the limits of my endurance and I said to myself, "To hell with 'em!" I told my wife to drop our windward anchor and then, a few moments later, she let the leeward one go, and we settled back for an hour of tugging and hauling as we evened up the scopes and positioned ourselves so that every skipper within fifty yards was unhappy. I knew I was in unfriendly territory when I heard the cheer that went up the moment I shut down my engines. We all then settled down into an uneasy truce and turned our eyes toward the harbor entrance to await the coming of the next performer.

It was at this point that I decided anchoring is 10 percent skill and 90 percent dumb luck. That had to be the reason it was such an ordeal to even the most experienced of skippers. The main difference between the beginner's efforts and the old sea dog's was that the old-timer accepted the fact that the whole procedure was a game of chance. He also knew that he didn't have to stand an anchor watch because all of his neighbors would be checking every boat's position in the event of a tide change or a sudden squall. That's why I prefer to have a beginner next to me. I know he'll be up and down all night, staring into the dark trying to figure out if he's dragging, and I'll hear his shouts of panic should we drift too close. The old salt will be snoring peacefully, relying on a nervous neighbor to warn him of impending disaster.

I suppose I've read as many articles and books on anchoring as any normal man and I've listened to heated discussions at many a yacht club bar on this subject, but I have yet to hear any two experts agree on which anchor holds best, whether chain or rope is preferable, how much scope is safest, whether to drop one or two anchors, and whether light, medium or heavy anchors and rodes work better than other combinations. If the experts can't agree, is it any wonder I get nervous when I get set to anchor?

Having embarrassed myself in many harbors, using a variety of anchor types and combinations of chain and rope, I now follow the simple procedure of dropping my anchor any damned place I please, giving it a tug to be sure it has taken some semblance of a bite, and then wrapping myself around a glass of Mount Gay rum. It may not be scientific, but it's easier on the old nervous system.

Once I'm snugged down, I protect my territory with every resource at my command. While I don't mind infringing on some other skipper's grounds, I become enraged the moment a new boat comes near me with the obvious intention of dropping anchor. I have a number of moves, graded from "Friendly Persuasion" all the way to the "War of 1812 Overture."

I start by standing on the foredeck wearing a frown and progress through a series of steps, depending on how stubborn the offending newcomer is. If a nasty look won't discourage him, I turn on my generator. I then move on to the "Victory at Sea" phase, which involves firing up the two diesel engines and turning up the hi-fi system.

If the fellow persists, I move on to the grand finale, which consists of switching on both radiotelephones, criticizing the man's motives on my loud hailer, bringing my dog on deck to bark as loudly as her sixteen-year-old vocal cords will allow, and having my wife hang a row of wash to dry on the rail.

Generally, the last I see of the intruder is the back of his head, enveloped in a cloud of diesel smoke, as he fumbles his way to the far corner of the anchorage. Strong measures, you say, just to assure privacy? Perhaps you're right. But no worse than I've been subjected to on many occasions. Nobody's ever made anchoring easy for me, and I think I'm a better skipper for it. So, I'm really doing the other fellow a favor.

I almost forgot a most important point. I always wave to the departing boat and wish them a happy day of cruising. After all, yachting *is* a gentleman's sport, isn't it?

A Hazard to Navigation

⚓ *DECEMBER, 1982*

During the late fifties, Dory and I lived in La Jolla and sailed out of the San Diego Yacht Club. Being a natural born trouble-maker, I got the idea of starting weekly races called the Twilight Series. The object was to gather together every Wednesday evening for a little fun and casual competition: each boat was to pick on another its own size and race out the harbor entrance, around a buoy and back. We had a turn-out of nine boats for the first race, and over twenty-odd years the number of participants has grown to as many as two hundred sailboats.

Now, it so happened that about the time that the racers were heading out of the harbor, the U.S. Navy ships were returning from their daily maneuvers. This created a traffic jam and some hard feelings on both sides. Some sailors, being independent souls, refused to give way, claiming the sail over power rule.

Since the club's inception, yacht club commodores have had to listen to the gripes of the Navy commanders. As the racing fleet grew, the problem became more serious. So, it was with considerable surprise that I read a letter describing me as a Hazard to Navigation, signed by the U.S. Navy Commander in San Diego. I didn't think the Navy had a sense of humor. The letter was presented to me during a fun-filled evening at the yacht club early in July.

Earlier, about thirty of us went storming through the Wednesday Night Beercan Race (as it is now called) aboard *Windward Passage*. Old friend John Rumsey, who is skipper, was in San Diego en route to Hawaii, and offered the boat for the race. Midway through the race, sure enough, a big Navy ship came in and docked, causing many groans among the fleet.

As for me, I suspect I am the only person ever designated as a Hazard to Navigation by the Navy. And to think that my father predicted I'd never amount to a hill of beans!

Who propelled the water balloon
onto the bridge deck of the *Constellation*?

COMMANDER
NAVAL BASE SAN DIEGO

RICHARD COLEMAN BRADLEY
LETTER OF RECOGNITION
June 30, 1982

The United States Navy has historically recognized major contributions by private citizens in the discovery of Hazards to Navigation. We take this occasion to recognize the contribution of Richard Coleman Bradley.

Mr. Bradley has contributed more to the creation of hazardous Navigation than all of the capes, rocks and shoals of geography; all of the hurricanes and typhoons of history; and all but the most recent and violent wars.

The Wednesday Night Beercan Race strikes terror in the bones of otherwise able and fearless ship commanders. The U.S. Navy Weapons Development Section is producing an air-to-ship rocket that will obsolesce the Exocet—it is called "The Beercan."

The dartboard in the Officer's Open Mess is replaced each July with the likeness of Richard Coleman Bradley, and is taken down each September tattered and unrecognizable.

The Chief of Naval Operations has ordered the C.I.A. to obtain, by any means, the plans for the catapult launcher that last August propelled a water balloon to the bridge deck of the *Constellation*, striking the Fleet Admiral behind the left ear. Such technology is vital to our nation in maintaining the balance of power.

On Wednesday night when our ships have all reported safely in, we dream of the peaceful and serene bygone days before Dick Bradley started the Beercan races.

Oh, God, how we wish he had been a golfer!

Paul T. Gillcrist
Rear Admiral, U.S. Navy

TWO

Beyond the Realm of Logic

Beyond the Realm of Logic

⚓ *MARCH, 1977*

Anyone who owns a boat is at least half nuts. Look around you next time you're at the yacht club or marina. Have you ever seen such a collection of crazies? Presidents of major corporations can be found kneeling in dirty bilges changing oil because they're convinced the yard won't do the job right. Doctors who earn $100,000 a year will cancel appointments with rich patients to discuss the merits of a sail with their favorite sailmaker. Women who regularly make the "best dressed" list can be found scrubbing bottoms wearing faded dungarees, torn sweatshirts and run-down Top-Siders. They're all out of their minds. But if you accuse them of being slightly off course, they give you a look that says, "You just don't know what it's all about, do you?"

Madison Avenue tries to base ad campaigns on logic. Hell, if a guy was logical he wouldn't own a boat at all. To be a true yachtsman you have to throw logic and common sense out the window and succumb to pure emotion. It's like when a man leaves his wife of twenty years, deserts his children, gives up his job and security, and loses the respect of his friends by running away to the islands with his nineteen-year-old girlfriend. Is it logical? Sensible? Reasonable? No, of course not! But it's life, my friends, and you know it. Emotion is the key. Emotion with a goodly dose of lust. The poor guy isn't a natural-born villain. He's a victim of his own emotions, the same way a man who falls in love with a certain boat has fallen victim to *his* emotions. Falling in love with a boat, like falling in love with a woman, is simply a case of temporary insanity. All you nuts line up on the right.

A fellow told me a story the other day about how Chevrolet did a lot of research on what the average American car buyer wanted in his next car. The overwhelming answer came back: "A basic black, four-door sedan with stick shift, no air-conditioning, no power brakes or steering, small economical engine and sturdy upholstery." They produced just such a car and nobody bought. The next year they did a similar survey, except this time they asked the people, "What kind of car do you think your neighbor would buy?" The answers were very revealing. "Oh, he's crazy. He wants a big, comfortable gas guzzler with a lot of pickup, fancy upholstery, power windows, and seats and steering, huge fins and automatic transmission. He's a real nut!" So the company built the neighbor's type of car and sold jillions of them. Never underestimate the opinion of a loony, some pundit once said.

I know a guy who'd been chasing his good-looking secretary around the office for a year with no success. Finally, he took her to a boat show, where he planned to order a new twenty-five-foot El Cheapo runabout. On the way to the El Cheapo display they passed a line of people waiting to board the Queen of the Show, an ostentatious sixty-five-foot yacht fisherman. Much against his will, he found himself standing in line for half an hour, pressed up against his lady love much of the time and growing more restive by the moment. Once aboard, she began to "ooh" and "aah" as she was led from one lavish cabin to the next. Then they came to the master stateroom. Throwing herself on the king-size bunk, she exclaimed, "Oh, Sweetie, I'd give anything to know a man with a boat like this!"

Two hours later my friend was the proud owner of a $165,000 yacht, a $115,000 mortgage, a greatly reduced bank account, and a future that meant moonlighting and eating franks and beans in order to keep up the payments. But his doubts were washed away as he felt his secretary's head on his shoulder, looked into her vacant blue eyes, and heard her throaty whisper, "Oh, Georgie, you're just too much." See what I mean?

And I'm just as goofy as the next guy. A few years ago my wife and I bought a boat without having seen anything except a couple of fuzzy Polaroid shots of it. On the day we inspected the boat, it was under full winter covers. It could have been a Sherman tank for all we could tell. The yacht-club tender took us out to where it was hanging on a mooring and we climbed aboard by lifting a corner of the heavy green canvas shroud. It was dark as a tomb in there, but we groped our way about, trying to figure out what it might look like in daylight. My wife worked her way down to the main cabin and inspected the galley with the help of a match. Meantime, I managed to squeeze myself under the canvas covering the cockpit. I sat behind the wheel and imagined myself sailing off to paradise. Lord, what an imagination! Finally, I called out to my wife, "What do you think?" She called back, "I like it." So we bought it that day—without a trial sail, I might add. I'd been told it was an S&S design. Which it was. I later found a set of plans signed "S&S. Suziki and Shibui, Tokyo."

Two years later we saw a thirty-eight-foot trawler, and thirty minutes after stepping aboard we had signed an order to have one built and delivered in New York. This was not unusual except that we lived in California and still owned our forty-one-foot S&S yawl. Until that fateful day we used to gargle with Listerine when the word "powerboat" sullied our lips. Emotion reared its ugly head and suddenly we were stinkpotters. Crazy? Of course. Was there ever any doubt?

Eventually, we sold the thirty-eight-footer and moved up to a De Fever 50 trawler, a luxurious piece of equipment that was totally beyond my ability to maintain, own, or handle. We decided to sell, but not until we'd found our next boat. We dread the thought of being boatless, even for a few hours. Perhaps we're afraid we'll discover how comfortable it is ashore. I don't know. Anyhow, we found a broker down in the Chesapeake and told him, "We want a forty-foot fiberglass cutter with an aft cockpit, high-performance fin keel and spade-rudder underbody, accommodations for eight while racing, and we are not interested in a cruising-type boat, so don't waste our time." He was smart. The first boat he showed us was a wooden forty-one-foot cruising-type ketch with an aft cabin, center cockpit, long keel and giant hooked-on rudder. That's as far as we got.

"It's perfect!" my wife said. "Exactly what we've always wanted."

Do you sometimes wonder why yacht brokers tend to drink heavily?

A couple of months ago we decided we'd had it with sailboats. Too much work and not enough comfort. So, back to power again. We gave the brokers a list of our requirements: heavy, 8 knots top speed, single diesel with the prop buried in the long keel, five-foot draft, economical (two miles per gallon), big sun deck opening directly from the main saloon, and a flying bridge. Tops of forty-feet overall length.

We bought the first boat we were shown. Can you guess? A fifty-two-foot Huckins cruiser with twin 216-hp diesels, top speed of 21 knots, burning twenty-one gallons an hour (that used to last me a month), no flying bridge, no sun deck leading off the main saloon, no . . . well, you get the picture. What makes us do these things? Emotion. That plus the fact that we're dedicated boating nuts. And the key word is "nuts."

How can I confess to such lunacy, you might well ask? Well, let me tell you. Practically every one of our friends are boat owners. Some of them are goofier than we are. They call it "enlightened." Whatever. I'm not about to change or worry about it because we have more excitement and laughs in a day than those poor souls on Madison Avenue have in a year. Sure, we know we're driving them up the wall. Maybe that's part of what makes us do what we do, the knowledge that we're not part of the mold, not predictable, not understandable by normal standards.

Like someone once said, "Anybody who loves boats and hates normalcy can't be all bad."

Animals (the Four-Footed Kind) on Board

⚓ *MARCH, 1980*

A couple I know recently returned from a three-year cruise in the Caribbean. The minute they tied up to the dock, she stepped off the boat, and he tossed her bags ashore, and another nautical romance had foundered on the shoals of "cabinitis."

She later described him as being an "animal" while he assured me she was a "dog." They were both mistaken. Their problems didn't stem from the fact that they were animals. The problem was that they *weren't* animals. Having cruised for fifteen years with a small dog named "Susie," I can guarantee you that any animal (excluding horses, cows, and buffaloes) makes a better cruising companion than a human.

Susie was a small white shaggy mutt my wife rescued from the San Diego dog pound. During the years she cruised with us in southern California waters, up and down the eastern seaboard and, finally, the Bahamas, Susie was the perfect guest. She was the daintiest of eaters, didn't touch a drop of my best booze, didn't smoke or chew tobacco, never complained about the weather, the seas or the course we were on. When she had to go, she let us know with a very small whimper. If we couldn't get her ashore, she had learned that it was permissible to use the foredeck. At those times she turned her back to us and went about her business in a ladylike fashion, holding her head high and retaining her dignity throughout the procedure.

After a while, Susie became a member of the family, and our two daughters introduced her to their friends as "Susie Bradley." There would be presents under the tree at Christmastime for her and cards would arrive from friends addressed to Dick, Dory, and Susie Bradley. If all this sounds a little crazy to you, so be it. But we'd had dozens of weekend guests aboard our boats over the years who would never be allowed to set foot on a vessel of ours again. We'd had guests who had consumed gallons of Chivas Regal and Jack Daniel's, eaten pounds of rare steak, snubbed dozens of cigarettes into gleaming varnish, and stopped up heads with a variety of unflushable items. Susie was innocent of all such acts of selfishness and thoughtlessness for her entire sixteen-year life-span.

When we left California for the East Coast, Susie was left in our older daughter's care for a few months. When we returned to California to pick her up, Dory refused to have Susie fly, having read about dogs freezing to death on commercial flights. There was no way she was going to turn over Susie's well-being to an airline. We solved the problem by buying a ten-thousand-dollar motorhome, which we needed like a second navel. From then on, when people asked me how much we had paid for Susie, I answered, "Ten thousand and five dollars, five dollars for the dog and ten thousand to get her from California to Florida."

Because we lived aboard for ten years, Susie became well known along the waterway and in the islands. Dockmasters and boating couples would greet her like an old friend and we once estimated that some five hundred pounds of steak had been given to us for Susie. About half of it reached her plate. I got the rest. She knew what I was up to, of course, but true to form she never uttered a critical word.

As Susie neared her sixteenth birthday, she began to fade rather rapidly. Finally, with her eyesight and hearing both gone, she fell overboard one night and I broke the fifty-yard-dinghy-rowing record all to hell. But we knew then that the time had come to let her leave this uneasy world with dignity. We took her to a kindly vet in Marsh Harbor, in the Abacos, and there she left us. It wasn't an easy decision to make because Susie had been a good cruising companion for a long time, a member of the family, and a loyal friend. We like to think of her asleep on the slope of a hill overlooking the clear water and sandy beaches of the Bahamas, a cruising ground she enjoyed as much as we did.

I realize you may be one of a large contingent of cruising people who think animals don't belong on boats. It's true that animals are a responsibility and often a nuisance. But the same can be said for people. The big difference is that an animal has the good sense to know when you want to be alone. Many's the night our Susie snuggled up alongside me as I read a book or took a turn at the wheel, silent with my thoughts and wanting only to be left alone. She'd sense my mood and plop down alongside me with her chin resting on my lap. She didn't bore me with idle conversation or cause me to worry with complaints, or question my judgment. She was just there, assuring me that she felt she was in good hands.

I swore when we left the Abacos that we'd never have another pet aboard. Not that I didn't like animals, but because I was convinced we'd never find another Susie. And we'd reached an age when we wanted to do more traveling by train and plane. But mostly it was because I was afraid I'd be comparing any new pet with Susie and the newcomer might not measure up to those high standards. And for about a year we were petless, although it sometimes took a firm stand on my part to keep Dory from bringing home a stray mutt she'd found wandering the neighborhood. But the time finally came when fate stepped in and took control.

A tiny stray kitten got separated from her mother and found her way onto the parking lot next to our boat. We had heard it whining for a day or two but couldn't locate it. Finally, we tracked the kitten down and discovered it was hiding in the muffler system of a parked car. With some effort and ingenuity, a friend of ours, Patsy Bolling, managed to climb under the car and rescue a tiny ball of fur that was scared out of its mind. She delivered the shaking creature to Dory, who immediately diverted her attention from me to the kitten, lavishing care and food and milk and love on it. I, meanwhile, was muttering that I had nothing against kittens except they tended to grow up and become cats.

I've always considered cats to be cold, haughty, indifferent to humans and not too much in the way of good cruising companions. I have discovered the errors of my thinking. Our kitten, now grown into a cat, started out in life living with people. She hasn't had enough of a feline education to understand that her actions are not typically those of a cat. She is a combination of a dog and a small child wrapped up in a gray fur coat. She talks to us constantly and loves people, just as the owners of the boats on our dock love her. She visits them, stopping only long enough to bid a friendly good morning—and they look forward to her visits.

But that's really another story. Patsy, named in honor of her rescuer, has taken a firm position in the Bradley family. And this past Christmas she got her first presents under the tree and cards arrived addressed to Dick and Dory and Patsy Bradley.

I like to think that Susie would have enjoyed Patsy. They are alike in many respects, particularly in their understanding of our moods. Patsy will never replace Susie in our thoughts, nor should she.

She has established her own place and it is secure. And does she know it! Looking back over twenty-five years of boating and the couples we've cruised with, I can't honestly say any of them measured up to either Susie or Patsy.

In fact, I hope someday to find cruising companions I can tell, "You're terrific! You're almost as good as having animals aboard." But I'm not optimistic it will ever happen.

The Perfect Liveaboard Boat

⚓ *AUGUST, 1982*

Dissatisfaction keeps most of this country's industry going. You trade in a perfectly good automobile for a new one not because there is anything wrong with the old one but because you have become dissatisfied with it as a result of reading the ads for the new cars or because your neighbor just bought a new one or for some other equally ridiculous reason. The same thing applies to boats.

We changed boats every couple of years for one reason or another until we ran up a list of fifteen different boats over a period of twenty some years. We justified the changes by kidding ourselves into thinking the new boat was a big improvement over the old, but seldom found it a valid reason for having traded; nor was the excuse that our tastes had changed or that our life-style had taken a new twist. But whatever the reason, we convinced ourselves that a new boat would bring about a state of bliss. It didn't work that way.

Then we discovered an aging lady called *Simba* in a slip in Maryland on a cold, rainy day. At first glance she didn't seem to offer much chance of being anybody's dream boat. She was pretty well covered with what was later identified as spider caca. The interior decorating was not our cup of tea, the price was more than we could afford, and we still hadn't put our forty-one-foot sailboat up for sale, meaning we'd end up as two-boat owners for a while.

But *Simba* had a couple of things going for her that offset the negative aspects. For one thing, she was a Huckins. An old Huckins. Long, low, narrow and with all of the characteristics that set the older models apart from the run of the mill. Her wood hull was sheathed in fiberglass. The twin engines were well over the voting age but sounded strong; and the interior was painted off-white with just the right amount of mahogany trim to give it a lovely, old-fashioned appearance. But, best of all, *Simba* had a dining saloon that could be converted into an office for me. It took us all of five minutes to decide we had found our perfect liveaboard yacht at last.

How has it worked out? Well, we've been living on *Simba* full-time for over six years and have yet to find reason to consider a change. Each time we leave on a trip we look forward to getting back to familiar surroundings. After visiting friends on boats costing ten times what we paid for *Simba,* we come back and say, "We wouldn't trade our Huckins for anything we've seen yet." It's as though *Simba* had been designed with a couple like us in mind. Not that everyone would find her as perfect for living aboard as we do. She has some peculiarities that have taken awhile to grow accustomed to.

Take the bridge, for example. It doesn't have full-standing headroom. This means that we spend a good deal of our time warning guests to "Watch your head!" But it also means that we get better protection from rain than a normal-height roof would give. We have only one control station, under the above-described bridge, but it has all the protection of a belowdecks station and far more protection than a normal flying bridge. Besides, when docking or anchoring, I'm handy to the deck to help Dory. This is a plus that is worth its weight in gold. Well, lead, anyway.

Knowing that we would be spending all of our time in a warm climate, we wanted plenty of deck space and that we have. Our long foredeck is great for lounging and has a bench with a backrest. Our bridge deck is only half covered, providing space for lounging in the sun. And we have a fishing cockpit that opens up to allow total access to the engines. When cocktail time rolls around, we lounge under our hard top and enjoy a view unmatched by any other boat in the marina, regardless of size or price tag.

Down below, *Simba* is a bit on the unusual side. She has only one stateroom. But it is large, the bunks are wide, the two hanging lockers provide all the storage we need, and the head has a shower. A hatch directly over our bunks allows us to look up at the stars at night and to wake up to a brilliant blue sky. Stepping into our main saloon is a step back in time. It's not huge but it offers comfort for six people and more, if they don't mind sitting on the floor. My office doubles as our formal dining room and, with its fold-down bunks, serves as a guest cabin for those dear friends who stop by.

Dory's galley is aft on the port side and is about ten feet long. She has everything she needs to prepare gourmet meals except an interest in cooking. These days she prefers to eat in the restaurant here in the marina. But if she ever rekindles her interest in cooking, she has a propane oven, a big refrigerator, separate freezer, microwave oven, and a variety of gadgets I bought her over the years hoping she'd change her ways.

Then there are the strange sounds an old boat makes. Dory's hearing is more acute than mine and she is constantly waking me up in the middle of the night and asking me, "What is that noise?" It is annoying to say the least, particularly when it turns out that the sound she hears is water pouring through the hull or wires snapping and flashing. If it was left up to my hearing and my reluctance to get out of bed, we'd sink twice a week.

But while *Simba* is thirty years old (and in this day and age that's ancient), she suits our needs just fine and I can't for the life of me say why we would want to trade for a larger, newer, faster, sleeker, beamier boat costing ten times what we paid for her six years ago. What I'd really like would be to figure out a way to keep dry rot from appearing from time to time. And to get all three heads working perfectly.

Dory would like to find a varnish that lasts a full year and she'd give anything to figure out how to get me off my lazy butt and out on deck to help her with the painting and varnishing. Of course, she'll be thrilled when I get around to replacing some of the broken porthole glass. And maybe installing some of that sun-reflecting plastic.

So, here we sit. A couple of ancient mariners aboard an ancient yacht (by today's standards). The paint glistens and the varnish is as shiny as it is on any gold-plater in the marina, thanks to Dory's skill and energy. *Simba*'s plumb bow and businesslike lines identify her PT-boat heritage. She's not what you'd call a pretty boat but she has a style distinctly her own. And our satisfaction with *Simba* is strengthened when a big, new fiberglass beauty pulls into the next slip and the owner leans over the rail of his million-dollar yacht and says to us, "Pardon me, but isn't that a Huckins? She's a real beauty!"

At times like these I frequently wish I could reply, in all honesty, "Thank you, so is yours."

Living Aboard Is a State of Mind

⚓ *APRIL, 1977*

"It's like stuffing ten pounds of potatoes in a five-pound bag!"

That's the way my wife describes the process of moving from a house ashore onto a liveaboard boat. As you start eliminating cherished possessions because they won't fit or are too heavy or too fragile, doubts will begin to gnaw away at your confidence. At least once a day she will ask, "Do you think we're doing the right thing?" On the day you reluctantly concede that your prized stereo system will have to go, and your camera cases won't fit the space you had allotted, and the electric typewriter is fated for the garage sale, that's the day you'll answer her with a brief "No!"

The boat that looked so spacious when you first saw it begins to shrink in size as each box of "things I just can't do without" comes aboard. Finally, both of you realize there isn't a cubic foot of unused space aboard and you're faced with what to do with the mountain of cartons still piled on the dock. Grandma's console sewing machine, the grandfather clock, the comfortable old rocker, the pictures of the kids, the blender (no more piña coladas), the ironing board, the iron, most of your clothes, and all but a few of your books—all are destined for disposal.

This is traumatic enough in itself, but when you add it to the agony you've gone through in disposing of your furniture, your precious antiques, your treasured paintings, the bronzed baby shoes, your grandfather's moustache cup, the combination washer-dryer, the Hammond organ, and the Ping-Pong table, you've got yourself a man-sized portion of panic and doubt.

The situation wasn't helped when, right from the beginning, your friends and neighbors did their best to discourage you from making a move which was, to them, foolhardy. Much head shaking greets the man who announces he is planning to give up the old homestead in favor of a lighthearted life at sea. "You'll be sorry" is the most oft-heard comment. "You gotta be outa your mind" is a close runner-up, while "I hope you know what you're doing" comes in third. The rest of the folks will just smirk and make snide comments.

The important thing is to remember that your move is more traumatic for your friends than it is for you. Your decision says, in essence, that everything *they* believe in, everything *they've* worked years to achieve, all *their* earthly possessions, all *their* minor accomplishments are nothing.

Your decision forces them to question not just your chosen lifestyle, but their own. This is something they've never thought about before. People don't like to be shaken up. They like to feel that, sure, life is rotten, but it's rotten for everybody. By proving to them that there may be something better, short of heaven, you're destroying their complacency and their faith in the American System. So, don't get mad at them. Understand them. But ignore them.

Once you've left the house and your friends behind, keep in mind that everything you write to your old friends will have impact on them. Those you love should be told that the new life is not all that great. Hardships should be described in detail. These people must be given an opportunity to tell themselves that you were wrong and they were right. Why make a friend unhappy?

On the other hand, to those you dislike, this trip represents a great opportunity to get even. Send them postcards describing a life that could be equaled only in paradise. Describe how much fun you are having, how many interesting people you have met, how cheap it is to live this romanatic life. They'll come to dread hearing from you, and each card will drive another needle in where it stings the most. Beautiful! How many times in life do you have a chance like this to return all of those snide remarks, all those affronts, all those slights and put-downs? Not many, so don't miss your chance. Depending on the depth of your dislike, you can keep it going for years. I still enjoy writing a nice chatty letter to a couple of characters I know. Under the guise of an update to a friend I manage to drive these characters up the wall as I could never do before.

Okay, so you've got everything on the boat that will fit and you've turned your back on the junk left on the dock. Now comes the time to stow your belongings. In your eagerness to get moving you decide to just find temporary places to store things. "We'll organize it later on," you tell one another. As a result, you spend the next two years moving stuff from one location to another. This is generally the wife's job, and it means that the man never does know where anything is located. He spends two hours trying to find his tool chest in the lazarette only to discover that his wife has moved it to the chain locker. A week later he tears the chain locker apart only to find his wife has moved it to a locker behind a settee.

This may sound trivial, but it plays a big role in how long a boat stays with one owner. After a while the frustrated skipper begins to hate his boat because he seems to spend most of his time searching it for things he thought he knew the locations of. In fact, there are wives who have been known to use this method to influence their mates to buy a larger boat, sell the sailboat and buy a big cruiser, or even get out of boating altogether.

Moving up to a larger boat so "we'll have space for all of our things" is a snare and delusion. The cheapest thing you can build into a boat is space, the most expensive is storage in the form of drawers, lockers, and cabinets. Hence, when you get your roomy new boat you find it may actually have less space for storage than your old small boat. Older boats had oodles of built-ins because owners demanded lots of cabinetwork and boat builders took pride in it. New boats have a minimum of fine cabinetry because newcomers to boating don't know what to expect and there aren't that many craftsmen around anymore. What you find in today's big boats is lots of air. But don't despair. Once you get to a marina, you can find a competent freelance carpenter who can build in whatever you need to store your goodies—and at less than you'll pay to have a builder or yard build them in.

As anyone who has owned both sailboats and powerboats can tell you, sailboats generally have more storage in proportion to their overall size than powerboats. When we moved from a forty-one-foot sailboat to a fifty-two-foot powerboat we found that we couldn't add much because both had the same cubic footage of storage. Well, almost the same.

Generally speaking, the trick is not to buy a larger boat. It is to reduce your possessions to the essentials. Just as achieving satisfaction is not necessarily increasing your income. Cutting back on your wants is a faster and more effective way to achieve happiness, particularly if living aboard a boat is included in your scheme of things. Of course, each person has his own idea of what is a necessity and what is a luxury. For example, we know people who are very comfortable and totally satisfied without a water-pressure system, refrigeration, air-conditioning, auxiliary generator, TV, soft bunks, range with oven or any number of amenities that my wife and I thoroughly enjoy. We've done without all of those fancy gadgets and been happy. We now have all those gadgets and we're even happier.

For example, a necessity to me is a blender with which to make a piña colada on a hot evening in the Bahamas. Call me a hedonist if you like. But last spring I spent six weeks in the islands drinking warm drinks made from rum and Tang. I loved every one and enjoyed myself immensely. But I know I'll have even more enjoyment each time I hear that blender whirring away, making a frothy drink that will slide down my gullet and bring cooling delight every inch of the way. So, let's not forget to put aboard the things that make your life complete, regardless of what old salts may advise.

As exhausting and traumatic as a move from a shore base to a boat may be, an even worse situation is where you move from a big, roomy boat to a smaller one. Here's a case where you've already eliminated everything in life that isn't absolutely essential to your existence. Suddenly you're asked to make a further sacrifice. Your wife stands on the dock, tears in her eyes, and pleads with you to say it isn't so. Surely, she is telling you, there's room for some of the little fancies she loves so much. This is the time for you to stand firm and remind her that she may be losing a few drawers but she's gaining the comfort that comes with owning a boat without a mortgage.

Perhaps the worst situation is where you move from one coast to the other while moving from a large boat to a small boat. I've heard stories where women have broken down completely and strong men have been known to cry. The only saving grace of such a move is that much of the decision-making is made for you. The movers frequently lose or destroy much of what you had planned for the boat, and this means that all you have left to move aboard is what they didn't drop or misplace.

Over the years we have moved many times, from small to large to small. We've moved from land to sea and back to land. We've moved from one coast to the other. We've lost many treasured pieces and also gained a few items that came from unknown sources. We've suffered the aches and pains that come with moving aboard. We've known the frustrations of trying to stuff ten pounds of potatoes into a five-pound bag. We've said on many occasions, "This is it. We'll never change boats again."

But time heals all wounds and blurs all memories. After a while one or the other of us will say, "You know, I really love this boat. But I saw a seventy-two-foot Grimsby in perfect condition the other day. The owner is really anxious to sell and he'll take this boat in trade. What would you think of . . . ?"

In Defense of Wooden Boats

⚓ *JANUARY, 1979*

People who like old wooden boats are an endangered species and I think it's a crying shame. Worse, they aren't being driven away by a deficiency on the part of the boats, they're just tired of having to defend themselves and their devotion in a world dedicated to aluminum, steel, fiberglass, and ferro-cement. Mind you, some of my best friends own boats built of something other than wood. My own youngest daughter and her husband live on a fiberglass sailboat and I have never covered up this information or denied their existence. Nobody can point the finger at me and accuse me of being a bigot. An old fogey, or a stubborn old mule who refuses to progress with the rest of the world, but a bigot? Never!

It's not bad enough that I like wooden boats, I happen to like *old* wooden boats. One reason being that the only boat I can afford is an old wooden boat, particularly if I'm going to own one big enough to provide Dory and me with enough space to live in relative harmony. Another reason is that experience has taught me that a well-built older wooden boat is a better investment than a poorly built new boat, whether it is built of wood, steel, or what have you.

There are those who accuse me of waffling because my present boat is built of two layers of mahogany sheathed in fiberglass. I say it qualifies as an old wooden boat and proudly show the builder's plaque stating *Simba* was built by Huckins in Jacksonville, Florida, in 1952.

During my two years of ownership, I've climbed into every nook and cranny of *Simba* and have detected not the remotest sign of dry rot, wet rot, or deterioration. I haven't found one single instance of poor design or skimping to save a penny, because back in 1952, quality was more than just a much-abused word. Does this mean I will never have dry rot problems? Of course not. But none has shown up in the first twenty-six years and I have good reason to believe there won't be any when *Simba* celebrates her fifty-second birthday.

Just ahead of me on the dock here on Fort Lauderdale's New River is a thirty-seven-foot Alden ketch built in 1929. It is beautifully maintained and its owners, who bought *Bonanza* some twenty years ago, are planning a Bahamas cruise this winter in complete confidence. Next is an Angleman thirty-six-foot ketch built about twenty years ago and in mint condition. The owner could set sail tomorrow for the South Seas without worrying about the ketch's ability to take it.

Two slips down from her is a lovely fifty-seven-foot Trumpy close to thirty years old. Her brightwork gleams and her decks are golden and she is every bit the queen of the marina.

Mixed in with this collection is a fiberglass sailboat of the type some refer to as the "suppository school of design." It looks a bit out of place among the floating antiques, but its owners are very nice and we wooden boat owners treat them as first-class citizens.

As any wooden-boat owner can tell you, the most oft-heard question is, "Doesn't the maintenance kill you?" In my case, I can truthfully answer that it doesn't, because my wife takes care of it.

The concern about time and money needed to maintain a wooden boat puzzles me. Most of the old cockers who worry about the time haven't anything but time on their hands anyway. You'd think they'd be overjoyed at having a reason to get up in the morning other than to go to the bathroom. As for maintenance costs, you could maintain a wooden boat for fifty years with what you'll save on the purchase price.

For example, my fifty-two-foot cruiser would cost about $375,000 to duplicate today. I got it for less than $60,000. That leaves me $315,000 to spend on maintenance before I hit a break-even point.

Of course, how much you spend on maintenance depends on how well the boat was built in the first place. I owned two Japanese-built trawlers that began falling apart from dry rot within a year of launching. They were built in 1970 and 1973 and their present owners keep them afloat by stuffing hundred-dollar bills into their punk parts.

I'm not saying you should buy a wooden boat if you have the wherewithal to afford a new aluminum or fiberglass one. I am advocating that you consider an older wooden boat if you find your budget confines you to a tiny, cramped craft of modern, maintenance-free materials. I feel sorry for people who spend their time edging around one another in a too-small cabin—all in the name of freedom from maintenance. Every boat needs some maintenance, regardless of the material from which it is built.

When the day comes to look for that retirement boat and you discover that your pocketbook doesn't allow the purchase of a shiny new floating palace, turn to your yacht broker and tell him to find you a graceful old girl that'll take you south to the sun in safety, comfort, and dignity and leave you enough in the bank to pay your fuel bill. You'll be amazed at the bargains lurking in his files.

The Boat Beyond

⚓ *FEBRUARY, 1981*

It is man's nature to be dissatisfied. Which explains why so many people attend boat shows, read boat ads and drive thousands of miles in search of a boat that is just a bit better than the one they have.

I thought I'd outgrown that urge to change for the sake of change. I was wrong. I'm as susceptible to the lure of a shiny new boat as any beginner. And I doubt if I'll ever outgrow that itch to board a new boat and compare it with what I have. That explains how I got myself into the state of agitation I now find myself enduring. And it explains why Dory keeps looking at me and saying, "You never learn. You just never learn!"

It all started a couple of months ago when I saw an ad for a new thirty-nine-foot sailboat with accommodations meant for two. I mentioned to my bride that this looked like the kind of sailboat we'd always wanted. She simply looked at me and said, "I don't want a sailboat. I want the boat we have." I tried to explain why I thought this particular sailboat had certain features we might find perfect for doing some cruising in the Bahamas when I gave up the treadmill I am on. Once again she gave me a baleful glare and said, "Forget it. I'm not moving onto a cramped sailboat now or at anytime in the future. And I don't care to discuss it further."

I was careful not to mention it again, but I hadn't put that thirty-nine-footer out of my mind. Not by a long shot. I'm like an elephant: fat, slow, clumsy, and blessed with a long and vindictive memory. So, when Dory and I found ourselves at the Norwalk Boat Show, I managed to lure her aboard the object of my intentions. She looked around with a suspicious expression on her face and then began to take an interest. I waited patiently for her to make comments.

"It certainly is amazing for just thirty-nine feet," she said. "See how light and cheerful it is? The cabinetwork is beautiful, too. And the main cabin is really roomy. And look at those huge windows. My, I wish this boat had been available when we were still in sail."

Then I made my first mistake. "Well, there's no law that says we can't go back to sail. It would be a lot cheaper to cruise than our present boat. And we always did like sailing."

Dory gave me a disgusted look and said, "If you recall, the last time we lived on a sailboat you drove me crazy. You worked in the main saloon and you had the whole place littered with your typewriter, paper, carbons, files, and other junk. No thanks. I'll stay with *Simba*."

"But what if I promised to be neat and tidy, and keep everything in its proper place, and put it all away at night so you wouldn't see it?" I walked into that one, but I had to try something.

"You never put anything away in your life. Face it, Bradley, you were born a slob. Your mother warned me about you before we were married. But I didn't listen. I figured you were going to be rich and I would have maids and a butler. I was wrong and your mother was right. You are hopeless when it comes to keeping a boat neat."

I changed tactics. "But I'm thinking of you, dear. This is a fiberglass boat and will be easier for you to keep clean. And with less space I won't be able to bring so much junk aboard. And we'll be in the islands, cruising from one snug cove to the next. It could be a wonderful life."

"It could," she replied, "but not with you. In the first place, you can't stand to be away from a phone for more than a day. If you don't check your mailbox every morning you have a fit. You are a telephone and mail junkie. You're a workaholic. You actually *love* what you are doing and you'll be typing away the day the world ends. You aren't going to change; you're getting worse in your old age."

Well! That's a helluva way for a man's wife to talk to him after forty-one years of busting my pick to give her everything she could ask for. But down deep I suspected she was right. I am prone to sloppiness in my thinking, my planning, and my work habits. We've got a fifty-two-foot powerboat with a ten-foot by twelve-foot cabin set up as my office. Every morning we go through the piles of paper on my desk and on the floor around me and try to make sense of it. By ten in the morning I have a neat desk and the floor is relatively free of mess. But by the end of the day it looks like a hurricane swept through an accountant's office. It is total chaos.

"You're right," I admitted. "But I have been thinking about slowing down. You know, stop spending so much time at the typewriter and taking it easier. Possibly help you maintain the boat and maybe do a few repairs here and there. You know, stuff that even a klutz like me can handle."

With that she patted me on the head and smiled. "Sweetie, why can't you face up to what you are? You are a busybody. You love to meddle in other people's business. You try to tell your readers how to live in your column. You try to tell your advertising clients how to run their businesses. You couldn't exist without your shiny IBM Selectric and a stack of blank white paper next to you. Am I right?"

She had me. That's what comes from not trading in wives every few years. "Okay, so you know me better than I know myself. But does that mean I have to stop dreaming about buying a new boat?"

"Of course not. You can dream all you want. And I think this is a lovely sailboat. I could be very happy living on it. But not with you. I can see myself cruising the islands with a tall, virile young fellow who could handle the sails alone, anchor alone; who never messed up the cabin; who loved to cook and fish and swim and beachcomb and had a beautiful singing voice and played a guitar and had inherited a bundle of money. Under those circumstances I could picture myself on this gorgeous sailboat. But there'd only be one small problem."

"What's that?" I asked.

"Sooner or later, this young fellow would have to stop singing long enough to say something. And that's when I'd get into the Zodiac, start up the old Evinrude, and head for the nearest airport. I'd hightail it back to Fort Lauderdale and I'd grab a cab and say, 'Get me to the yacht *Simba* at the Riverside Hotel and hurry!' "

I was really flattered. "You mean you'd give up all that just for me?"

Once again, she patted me on the top of the head and said, "You bet your bippie. I realized a long time ago that my role in life was to see to it that you didn't drown in a sea of paper and typewriter ribbons. I guess I'm in the same position as that fellow who made a career out of following the elephants around the circus. When he was asked why he didn't find a better job, he said, 'What? And give up show biz?' "

As she stepped up into the cockpit she said, "However, if you want to show me that sixty-one-foot motor yacht over there, I'd be willing to hear your arguments for changing boats."

Giving the sailboat a last longing look, I replied, "No thanks, dear. I'm out of the mood."

But someday I'll try again.

The Summer of Our Discontent

⚓ *NOVEMBER, 1980*

Did you have a nice summer? Did it go too fast for you? Was it hot enough for you? Good! I'm happy for you. Mine was lousy, thanks. How, you might ask, could a person not enjoy spending a summer in Newport, Rhode Island, during an America's Cup year? Believe me, it ain't easy. You have to work at it or make some bad decisions along the way. We ruined our summer by making just one wrong decision. We decided to leave our floating home, a fifty-two-foot Huckins cruiser, in Fort Lauderdale while we spent four months ashore, living in a comfortable apartment. That was it. That was the mistake and it's one we'll never make again.

It seemed so perfect at the time. We'd have lots of room for our younger daughter and our grandchild to live with us. There'd be room for our older daughter to spend weekends with us. There'd be hundreds of friends passing through Newport during the summer. Yes, we told ourselves, this may be the best summer we'll ever have.

The first couple of weeks went by and we actually enjoyed living on land. We liked the big rooms of the apartment we'd rented for the summer, the third floor of a big old mansion. The huge electric range and oven and the big refrigerator were welcome novelties. The freedom from checking bilges and batteries was a blessing. Our location just a few blocks from the center of America's Cup action appeared to be ideal. I had one huge room for my office and nothing to distract me from my work. No passing boats. No people hollering at me as they sailed by. No giant yachts throwing wakes within a few feet of *Simba* as they headed upriver to a yard. It was the perfect place to start that novel I'd been thinking of.

About the third week I found myself getting edgy. I wasn't coming up with any ideas, my novel wasn't going well, I'd run dry on subjects for my column, and more and more I found myself wanting to take a stroll down to the waterfront. By the end of the second month Dory, my wife, and I both knew that something was wrong. We were taking long walks and running into old friends and reading a lot and telling ourselves that things were great, but both of us knew we were simply putting up a good front. Down deep we were discontented and the reason for our discontent was the fifteen-hundred-mile distance between us and our boat. It was as simple as that. For a while we told each other it was because we couldn't see the water. But then we babysat a lovely home overlooking the water for friends of ours and after a couple of weeks of that we both said, "This is a lovely home in a beautiful setting and it is everything a person could ask for in a house. But it has one major drawback. It isn't a boat. Specifically, it isn't *our* boat."

It's September as I write this and we are making plans to leave the cool and refreshing breezes of Newport and start working our way back to the heat and humidity of Fort Lauderdale. We're boat-sick. We want to be *on* the water, not near it. We want to feel it under us, smell it, and taste it in the air, watch it flow past us, thrill at the sight of giant tarpon leaping from it in pursuit of mullet. We have discovered once again that normal living may be fine for the multitudes, but it doesn't suit the Bradleys. We are hooked on the liveaboard life and we might as well face up to it.

A dear friend called this morning. Bim Newcomb, who, with his beautiful wife, Mila, lives aboard a forty-foot cruiser in Florida and the Bahamas. "We're driving up and down the East Coast looking for a place to settle down. We've put the boat up for sale and we want to be able to buy a home when we say good-bye to *Sand Dollar*."

"I know just what you're going through, Bim," I told him. "Dory and I go through the same thing once a year. The best cure is to find a real-estate broker and start looking at houses. Three or four days of being shown run-down shacks in seamy neighborhoods at prices far beyond our reach generally jolts us back to reality. But if that doesn't work, ask yourself a few questions."

"Like what kind of questions?"

"Well," I said, "ask yourself who you'll talk to when you're living in that cute little farm town in North Carolina. How many of your old friends will be stopping by for a drink if you move into a condominium in Colorado? Picture yourself up to your butt in snow during the winter months when the new owner of *Sand Dollar* is lolling around on the deck in a pair of swim trunks, sipping a cool rum concoction while ogling a scantily clad maiden on the next boat."

"Wait a minute, old friend," he protested. "You forget that I'm getting along in years and my eyes are not too sharp for picking up buoys."

"If you're in that bad shape you don't belong in a car on land, colliding with people and trees. At least at sea you can't hurt anyone but yourself, and then only if you run aground. Besides, if you sell your boat for forty thousand dollars you'll end up with a dump in a bad area and you will never forgive yourself. When you get too old to live on a boat, you're too old to live . . . period."

"By God, you're right," Bim said. "I've known that all along but I've let Mila influence me into thinking we needed a place for our Persian rugs, Chippendale furniture, and other such trivia. See you on the river, pal."

"Who was that?" Dory asked. "Were you meddling in somebody's life again?"

"No," I answered. "I was just advising Bimmy not to sell his boat and buy a house. He thinks that just because he's seventy-one he should be ashore."

"Well, Bradley, for once in your life you've done right. I don't want to move ashore until I'm at least ninety. And then I'll go screaming and kicking. And if I discover heaven isn't located on the water, I don't intend to accept the invitation."

As I said, this was our summer of discontent. But it will be our last. Land is a great place on which to grow vegetables and old people. The sea is for young people, regardless of age. Salt water is the finest preservative known. If you're smart, you'll make good use of it.

Sex and the Single Hull
⚓ *SEPTEMBER, 1977*

According to my sources, two recent surveys have caused great concern. One is a study conducted by the National Institute of Child Health and Human Development that shows teen-age sex is on the increase, while the other indicates that sexual relationships between married persons who live aboard boats is on the decrease.

Obviously, the wrong people are having all the fun.

Boating people have reacted to the second study, which shows that a married couple's sex life diminishes as middle age combines with the discomforts of a narrow bunk. Another influencing factor is the tendency for women to suffer from motion sickness as they mature; thus a round-bottomed boat that rolls is less suited for married bliss than a hard-chined vessel that reacts less violently to wakes of passing boats. This problem of seasickness is serious, as anyone who has tried to woo a woman with a green face can attest.

I happen to live in a Florida marina that boasts a wide range of ages and marital situations. When I read the results of the survey I decided to conduct my own. The study covered a period of four months and details the sex lives of young unmarried couples living on small sailboats, young married couples living on slightly larger sailboats, and middle-aged couples with young children living on forty- to forty-five-foot sailboats and small powerboats. It is obvious to me that those who have the greatest need for room, comfort, and privacy have the

A study was done on sex life
on board small, medium and large boats.

least, while those who have little need for these luxuries are wallowing in king-sized double bunks, spacious aft cabins, and yachts whose deep draft and wide beam keep motion to a minimum.

Oddly enough, everyone was willing to discuss the topic with me and I include a few comments made by those I interviewed.

Sam Johnson shares a twenty-three-foot fiberglass sloop with a comely young girl who is simply introduced as "Nubbins." When asked if he found the narrow berths and lack of headroom in his boat to be a deterrent to sex, he replied, "Whaddaya mean, lack of room? We use one of the bunks for sail storage and sleep in the other. Who needs headroom? When we wanna stand up we get off the boat. Ain't that right, Nubbins?"

Nubbins appeared to be a little distracted by a strange cigarette she was smoking but otherwise eager to be helpful.

"That's right," she said. "Everything's cool except I keep getting black-and-blue marks in the strangest places. Here, take a look." I could see what she meant.

Fred and Cynthia Cogswell live on a forty-foot aft-cabin ketch with two young children. The Cogswells appeared to be in their mid-thirties and were relatively normal in most respects. I asked them if the aft cabin contributed to marital bliss.

"It helps," Fred Cogswell told me. "But it isn't perfect by any means. Whenever we feel the need to be alone, we lock the door to the aft cabin. But this makes the dog (a black Labrador weighing some seventy pounds) howl, the kids start crying, the neighbors complain about the noise, and the neighbors' kids race over to peek in the portholes. As I say, it isn't perfect but we're starting to get used to it."

"Does the rocking of the boat disturb you?" I then asked Mrs. Cogswell.

"No, but it sure seems to bother the people in the next slip," she replied.

As it turned out, the people she referred to were Mr. and Mrs. John Plompton, in their early forties and the parents of a teen-age daughter. I asked why they were disturbed by the motion of the boat in the next slip.

"Wouldn't you be disturbed if you were trying to raise a fifteen-year-old girl? What with the boat rolling, the kids crying, the dog howling, the kids peeking through the portholes, and the rest of the folks on the pier cheering them on, how am I supposed to keep my daughter from getting interested in sex? What's really annoying is the happy grins those two wear when they finally come up on deck. Disgusting!"

I then brought up the survey that showed that her teen-age daughter was probably enjoying sex right at that very moment.

"No way," Mrs. Plompton assured me. "She's running around with a boy who lives on a thirty-seven-foot sloop on the next pier. There's no way those two can make out on that boat. In fact, that's one reason we moved aboard. We figured a marina was the safest place to raise a young girl."

"But just for precaution, don't you think she should take the Pill?" I asked.

"We mothers in the marina have found a better system than the Pill and it doesn't have side effects. We just hide the Dramamine. It works like a charm."

When I inquired about their own sex life, they assured me that they were beyond sex. "We're into Transcendental Meditation," Mr. Plompton told me. "In this hot climate we find it's just as much fun and we don't perspire as much."

Mrs. Plompton concurred. "John is right. Before we got into TM he was a beast. Always trying to hug me and kiss me. Why, he even tried to get me to see a blue movie one afternoon. Shocking for a Ph.D., wouldn't you say? But now, between TM, Valium, cold showers, elevenses, and this cramped miserable boat, our sex life is serene."

My studies led me to the conclusion that life was unfair. By the time a couple could afford the comforts and privacy that make sex a pleasure, they were too old to remember what it was that they had enjoyed so much. The twenty-year span between thirty and fifty, when a married couple should be enjoying their most intimate relationships, was wasted. The only ones who seemed to get their fair share of what life is all about were the young couples who lived on tiny boats.

When I told my wife I was going to do an article about sex on boats, her only comment was, "Oh? I didn't know you were interested in writing fiction."

Bradley's American Dream

⚓ *JANUARY, 1981*

As a friend of mine and I walked away from a boat show last fall, the conversation turned to the high cost of boats. My friend sounded quite bitter while I tried to justify the rising prices. But I wasn't getting too far with him and by the time we reached his car I had just about run out of arguments. Then I noticed his wheels.

"Wow," I said. "That's some fancy automobile. You must have paid a small fortune for it."

"Not really," he replied. "I got it for just under eighteen thousand dollars and I got a nice trade-in on my old car."

"You mean you paid eighteen thousand dollars for this thing and you have the nerve to complain about the cost of a boat? You've gotta be out of your mind." (I should mention I know this fellow pretty well.)

He spun around on me and said, "Wait a minute! What's the cost of this car got to do with the cost of a fifty-thousand-dollar yacht. I don't get the connection."

"Well, for one thing, let's talk about value. You've got a car that has already dropped about five thousand dollars in value since you drove it off the dealer's lot. It's already rusting away. A year from now half of those fancy electronic gimmicks you've got won't work. The chances are good that the government will make the builder recall the thing because it's a menace on the road. By next fall there'll be a new style change and you'll be itching to trade this in on next year's model. Five years from now this will be in a junkheap someplace. Is that what you call a good value?" (I should also mention that my big mouth loses me a lot of friends.)

"Okay, so maybe you're right," he admitted. "What's that got to do with the cost of boats?"

"For one thing, where your eighteen-thousand-dollar car will be a worthless pile of scrap iron in a few years, that fifty-thousand-dollar boat will still be going strong fifteen, twenty, maybe fifty years from now. And instead of losing money on it every year, the chances are damned good that that yacht will be worth more in fifty years than it is right now. Nobody knows how long a well-maintained boat will last. It might last forever!"

My hard-nosed friend gave me a disgusted look and said, "What boat did you ever see that was worth more than its original cost twenty years later? There ain't no such animal."

Aha, I had him there. "How about my own boat, *Simba*. Huckins built it in 1952 and it cost the original owner about seventy thousand dollars. I just turned down seventy-five thousand for *Simba* because it is as good today as it was the day it was launched. In fact, it's better because it was fiberglassed about ten years ago."

He roared with laughter and said, "Why would anyone pay you that much for a twenty-six-year-old boat? Why, you've probably re-powered it six times and still have worn-out engines."

"Oh no," I replied. "My engines are the original GM 6-71s that Huckins put in when they built the boat. And you know something? They run as smooth and as economically as they did in 1952. In fact, they seem to run smoother every year."

"Well, I've got a diesel engine in my car, so it may be running a long time from now." He figured he had me on that one.

"Forget it, pal. What you've got is a gasoline engine that smells like a diesel. Your engine has been programmed to self-destruct about the time your fenders have rusted off. But you know something? It isn't just how long a boat lasts or how it appreciates in value that is important. It's the difference a boat can make in your life that counts."

My friend's answer to that was, "Yeah, I know all about that. If I had a boat I'd have to sell my car. That's the big difference."

"That's exactly where you're wrong," I told him. "The most beautiful years of my life have been spent aboard boats. It wasn't until I bought a boat that I really got to know my kids. Until I bought my first boat, I spent my time on the tennis court and Dory spent hers developing a stiff neck watching me. But the day we both stepped aboard a boat, we knew we'd found a new and better way of life."

"You mean your kids like the boat? I'm not sure I could get my kids on board if I had one. They don't seem to like to be around me very much. Come to think of it, I can't even get my wife to spend a lot of time with me lately. But, hell, I'm under a lot of pressure at the office and I guess I'm not the easiest guy to be around when I'm tense or tired." My God, I'd never heard him admit to a single flaw before.

"Listen, you idiot," I said. "If you had a boat you could get away from the very crap that is making you nervous and tense and hard to be around. You could untie the lines and get out on the water and before you knew it the whole world would begin to make sense. There is nothing like floating on a bright blue sea under a friendly warm sky, a can of cold beer in one hand and the wheel of your yacht in the other, to make you feel that maybe . . . just maybe . . . God had something good in mind for you after all.

"And as for your wife and kids," I went on, "if you'd give them a chance to see what you're really like under all that macho executive façade you wear like a suit of armor, they might even come to like you. After all, your wife must have seen something nice about you when she married you."

I could see I'd gotten his attention.

"Hm-m-m, that does make sense. But what if I buy the boat and my wife is afraid to leave the slip."

"Don't worry about it. You'll have the best waterfront condominium you've ever seen. And the best neighbors you could ask for. And the best investment you could possibly make. And on weekends you can wear a funny cap with a lot of gold braid and a pair of rubber-soled shoes and a blue blazer. You can train your family to call you 'skipper' instead of 'the old grouch.' And you can brag down at the office about having spent the weekend on your yacht. Your boss will look at you with new respect. And your cute little secretary will start calling you 'captain.' And maybe she won't run so fast when you chase her."

Suddenly he turned around and said, "Have you got time to go back and look at that fifty-footer with me? Not that I'm really interested, you understand. But as long as I'm here, I figure what the hell."

I wish I could tell you the story came out exactly as I had said it would, but it didn't. He bought the fifty-foot yacht and his wife and kids discovered he was really not a bad guy. He looks great in his gold-encrusted cap and deck shoes and blue blazer. His boss gave him a raise and a better position. His family now refers to him as "the skipper." But his cute little secretary is still running as fast as ever and she still calls him "Old Horny" (after Captain Horatio Hornblower, no doubt).

But what the hell. He wouldn't know what to do with her if he caught her, anyway.

Act Now . . . Before Offer Expires

⚓ *JANUARY, 1982*

Boat shows are filled with dreamers . . . on both sides of the counters. On one side are the people who wander down the aisles and docks, looking at the glamorous products and dreaming of the day when they can afford to buy that bigger boat, that sophisticated piece of electronic gear or that gadget that would make the next cruise even more perfect. On the other side are the builders whose ability to make this year's payroll depends on making a sale and the gear manufacturers who are praying their new, spectacular and amazing product strikes the public's fancy. A boat show is a dream factory with success or failure riding on a toss of the dice.

Mixed in with the dreamers and procrastinators are the hard-eyed hull-thumpers, those couples who have tired of dreaming and have said to each other, "Now is the time to buy. We're not getting any younger, prices aren't getting lower, and interest rates are probably going to stay high or get higher. Let's do it now!" These are the lucky ones. These are the people who recognize that God or Mother Nature or the Fickle Finger of Fate doesn't issue non-cancellable contracts guaranteeing a long life or everlasting health and vitality. These are the wise few who have faced up to the unpleasant truth that "someday" may never come and that the future . . . *their future* . . . may be distressingly and even frighteningly short. It is on the shoulders of this minority of enlightened boat lovers that the health of the boating industry rests.

The rest of the crowd is made up of the dreamers who will never quite work up the courage to make the move and will spend the rest of their lives saying, "If only" and "We shoulda." When Dory and I go to a boat show we are approached by many couples who tell us that someday they're going to have all the kids in or out of college, money in the bank, Grandma in a rest home, peace in the world, and whatever else it takes to make them move. These are the same people who tell the salesmen, "But last year this same model was ten thousand dollars less." And they'll repeat that statement over and over again with each passing year.

I find it hard to talk to people like that. Perhaps it's because Dory and I have always lived as though there might not be a tomorrow. Our friends have always chided us for not saving for a rainy day or our old age or some other unpleasant situation. And we have always answered, "Hand us that non-cancellable contract that guarantees we'll live to see a rainy day or reach a doddering old age and we'll give your warning some thought. Meantime, we have to run because the yacht broker is waiting for us to sign an offer on a bigger boat."

When we left Chicago and headed west in a brand-new yellow Jeep pulling a twenty-one-foot trailer, our friends and business associates said, "You'll be sorry!" When we left La Jolla and moved to Palm Beach, Florida, we heard the same old refrain. Oddly enough, we have never been sorry. What do we have to be sorry about? We've lived in the most beautiful spots in the country, stayed there until Dory decided it was time to move on, and then picked another beautiful place to tie up our boat.

Dory and I have always set realistic goals, well within reach and requiring a limited amount of effort and agitation to achieve. At the tender age of sixty-six I find that I have reached every goal I set for myself plus a few that simply fell into the basket along the way. During the twenty-five years we've been in boating we've had sixteen different boats, both power and sail. Each was the perfect boat for that particular period of our lives. When we were ready for the next phase, we changed boats, just the way we changed locations. Six years ago we bought *Simba* and while we have moved around from one harbor to another, we've decided *Simba* is the right boat for the rest of our lives afloat.

We can look back on twenty-five years of great boating, great fun, great friends, and a life rich in experience and satisfaction. And we are quick to admit that much of the enjoyment and satisfaction we have gotten from life has come from the ownership of a boat. So, it's only natural that we feel a sense of pity for the folks we meet at boat shows who are quick to defend their boatless situation with a litany of, to them, legitimate excuses. Strange as it may seem to those of you who are familiar with my curmudgeonly personality, I find it difficult to brace them and ask the questions that are on the tip of my tongue.

So, dear boat-show shoppers and dreamers, here's a word of advice from Uncle Dick. Keep in mind that there ain't no such thing as a free lunch. Everybody pays for what he or she gets out of life. We are destined to lose in the long run, and if you've reached the ripening age of forty you're already past the halfway mark. From here on out you aren't going to improve a hell of a lot. As Satchel Paige said, "Don't look back. Something may be gaining on you." If a boat is in your future, remember that the future may consist of the next two years. The perfect moment to buy the boat of your dreams may never arrive. By the time you've got all of the problems solved and the future secure, you may be too old and tired to untie your dock lines or steer the boat. Worse yet, Mother Nature or the Fickle Finger of Fate may have plans for you that preclude sailing off to paradise for your sunset years.

Does this sound like a pitch to sell boats? It isn't. What it is is a pitch for you to buy that boat and make that dream come true so that two, five or twenty years from now you don't find yourself turning to your wife and saying, "If only . . ." and you don't hear her reply, "Yes, we shoulda . . ."

At Last, the Perfect Yacht

⚓ *OCTOBER, 1981*

Forty-three years ago, when Dory and I were married, she was a girl with rather modest ambitions. She wanted a baby, a dog, a nice apartment, and maybe a car someday.

Over the years her goals became a bit more grandiose, mostly due to my optimism. I was always on the verge of making that one big strike that would set us up for life. Our cars grew in size, and our

I took her cruising on a boat
that met her standards . . . and then some.

houses got larger and more impressive, and our boats got longer and more expensive. But then, a few years back, Dory sort of put a hold on her ambitions and her objective changed to maintaining the status quo.

"We don't need a bigger car. The VW is just fine.

"We don't need to make any more money. Just slow down and let's enjoy what we have.

"Of course a bigger boat would be nice, but I haven't seen one that is *that* much nicer."

And then I made the big mistake. I took her cruising on a boat that met her standards . . . and then some. In fact, when the time came to disembark, she tied herself to her bed. I would have complained except that I had tied myself to my bed, barricaded the door, and threatened to ask for asylum. Nothing worked and we finally left the ship, dragging our feet all the way, and shouting to the captain, "We'll be back. You wait and see. We shall return."

The cause of all this commotion was a graceful ship with the nickname of "QE2." Just the mention of it brings back memories of the six most elegant, luxurious, relaxing, hedonistic days of our lives. QE2: nine hundred thirty feet of steel and fine woods and fine upholstery and Cordon Bleu cooking and great wines and gracious service.

Get this: for every couple on board there was one crew member whose sole objective was to make certain his passengers were coddled, spoiled rotten, entertained, tummies filled, stimulated mentally, and subjected to the kind of attention normally accorded a premature baby. Dory lapped it up as though she'd been born to this luxury. I, not wanting her to wallow alone, joined her enthusiastically.

For the first couple of days we walked around wearing glazed expressions, a reaction to the menus. We were offered such goodies as five styles of eggs, bacon, sausages, fish, lamb chops, ham, roast beef, chicken, turkey, and scrumptious pastries.

A typical lunch offered eleven different appetizers, three soups, two kinds of fish, three types of eggs, three hot dishes, steak, vegetables, salads, cold plates, nine desserts, eleven kinds of cheese, and anything to drink that suited your fancy.

To further complicate things, during lunch we were handed dinner menus and asked to make our selection. When the maître d' came to take our dinner order he would also list goodies not on the menu. These might include duck à l'orange, rack of lamb, chateaubriand, and a few other exotic dishes. We were consistent in one regard—we started every dinner with Iranian caviar (a habit we had to drop the instant we disembarked).

When we weren't eating we were watching movies, napping, sunbathing on deck, napping, socializing with newfound friends, reading, having cocktails, napping, listening to interesting speakers (favorite was New York's radio talk-show host Barry Gray), enjoying tea and biscuits at eleven and four, napping, and getting psyched up for the next fantastic meal.

At night there was entertainment, dancing, movies, and a round of parties. Six days of that kind of life could ruin you forever. The truth of the matter is, Dory has not cooked a meal since we got back to *Simba*. When I ask her if she plans to cook on board, she answers, "No way!" When I ask her what appeals to her for dinner, she mumbles, "I'd like to start with caviar. And I'd like to be served by John and Tony." (Our waiters on the *QE2*. There were two super waiters for every four tables. Talk about service!) If I ask her if she'd like a drink, she says, "Call the wine steward." It's a little hard to convince her that before the trip *she* was the wine steward.

You may laugh, but it's a serious problem. It's reached the point where I have to prepare my own drinks. I even have to make up my own plate of cheese and crackers during cocktail hour. Last week I even had to make myself a sandwich for lunch. Me, who has been coddled and cared for all these years. What concerns me is what will happen when the time comes to start eating on board again. Will I be required to learn how to cook? I like to be treated like a king. I enjoy sitting in my helmsman's chair while Dory gets the coals started and puts the meat on and charbroils it to a turn. If she insists, I might take the steaks off the fire so that she can serve the vegetables. But that's about the limit of my cooking ability.

But now it looks as if the *QE2* has changed all that. I keep telling Dory we'll take another cruise on the *QE2* but in the meantime she has to get back to cooking. That's when she looks at me and says, "No, thanks. I'll just wait until we have John and Tony serving again. Meantime, you'll do quite nicely."

Company's Coming

⚓ *JANUARY, 1978*

A lot of people talk about buying a boat and getting away from it all. It's a great idea, but anyone who lives aboard knows it ranks right up there with Ptolemaic astronomy and grapefruit diets as a working theory.

For one thing, people who live on boats fascinate those who lead normal lives with 2.7 children on .85-acre suburban plots. Inside every Levittowner is a bit of the old Errol Flynn, itching to simplify his life and sail off to a deserted island. So when he wanders down a dock and finds people enjoying this so-called simple life, he feels compelled to squat down by the cockpit where they are trying to disassemble a fuel pump and say, "Howdy. Sure is a pretty boat."

Now in my case, dockside dreamers are a blessing. I've long suffered from the "lazies," a malady that malingers on. My wife is constantly after me to get off my duff and get something accomplished on the boat or at the typewriter, knowing full well that I'm not afraid of hard work—I've been fighting it for years. As she says, "I don't care what you do, just do *something.*" So I do—I chat.

Of course, chatter can be overdone. We tied up at a marina fronting a condominium complex for a couple of winters in Florida. There was a constant stream of owners and guests strolling down the docks and peering into our windows. Now I could understand their feelings. Living in a condominium project where everyone is between sixty-five and eighty and gets winded playing checkers is a depressing way to spend the autumn years. It's only natural that they should want to wander down the docks and look at the funny people living on boats. There they are at dinner time, four or five faces pressed against my windows. A quavering voice says, "Oh, look, Harold. They're eating dinner just like real people."

So far I've mentioned only the problems posed by strangers who

I live in constant terror of hearing
those spine-tingling words, "Ahoy aboard the *Simba*!"

think boat people are fair game. A far more serious problem is friends. Most liveaboards spend their winters in the south and summers in the posh watering holes of the idle rich. What could be more attractive than paying a surprise visit to good old Dick and Dory in Florida around the middle of February. Never mind that Dory spends the daylight hours sanding and varnishing and that Dick has a disposition like an untipped waiter.

Now the normal thing to do would be to call and wangle an invitation, but that's too chancy, and besides, it takes a long-distance phone call. No, much better to "pop in." I live in constant terror of hearing those spine-tingling words, "Ahoy aboard the *Simba!*"

If there's one thing I've learned, it's to face up to the situation immediately. There's no way to hide. I've tried. I've spent miserable hours crouched in the shower while guests scurried around, unpacking and settling down for the winter. On one occasion, Dory and I avoided discovery until our visitors left for dinner. Without hesitation, we piled their junk on the dock and took off for a month in the Bahamas. The quickest way to wipe out a friendship is to sponge on it.

Fellow liveaboards are rarely a problem. After a few years of making the Waterway trip, we have friends spread up and down the East Coast and throughout the Caribbean. The nice thing is that we don't see too much of them, because they're moving around just as we are. Maybe old Joe would steal a dead fly off a blind spider. Maybe his wife would starve to death if it weren't for the olives in her martinis. We'll never get to know them well enough to discover their bad points. Any life-style that prevents others from getting to know our less attractive personality traits should be encouraged.

Does all of this mean that it's impossible to get away from it all in a boat? Of course not. If you really want privacy, you can always find a few escape hatches. Try living aboard in Maine during the winter. Or stay tied to the dock in Florida through August. You won't entertain a doubt.

Or untie the lines and move a hundred yards away to a strange marina. For a few days you'll bask in the quiet and freedom from pesky friends. But careful! It won't be long until the joys of resetting the points and cleaning the injectors palls, and you ache for the interruption of a cheery, "Ahoy there on *Albatross!*" If it turns out to be a couple so dull they dye Easter eggs white, and you're happy—delighted—to see them, then you're hooked on the liveaboard life-style forever. Keep those conversations ho-humming.

· THREE ·

Cant They Leave Us Alone?

The Curse of the Cruising Canine

⚓ *JANUARY, 1977*

So you want to take your dog cruising? Can you do it? Of course you can. The question really is, "Do you want to?"

Let me draw a picture.

You've finally fallen into a dead sleep, exhausted from having set and reset the anchor four times during the night. You're totally oblivious to the driving rain and the wind howling in the rigging. Even the heeling of the boat with each new gust leaves you undisturbed. But then you dimly become aware of a most unwelcome sound, a whining that can mean only one thing. But you fight the thought and bury your head deeper into your pillow. Finally, you know you've lost as your wife nudges you and says, "Honey, are you awake? I think Beauregard has to go out."

You roll over and find yourself staring into the big brown eyes of your overweight, not-too-bright, fifty-pound Basset hound. His short, ugly legs are doing what he thinks is a dance, and that tells you you'd better move fast. So you force yourself out of bed, shrug into foul-weather gear, and risk straining your back hoisting Beauregard up

So you want to take your dog cruising?

through the companionway, across the slippery deck, and into a bobbing and very unstable dinghy. Then you look around and try to figure out just where in all that inky blackness is the nearest shoreline. Ah! During that flash of lightning you see a line of brush that seems to be land. Thank God it's downwind. You'll worry about getting back later.

You row into some low, overhanging branches and heave the dog onto what appears to be land. Beauregard hustles off on his stumpy legs into the bramble and you wonder what predators await him. Perhaps an alligator will find him a tasty morsel. At a time like this, thoughts run through your mind that normally would be dismissed as depraved. You give him a decent interval to accomplish his mission and you call and whistle in an effort to get him back. No luck! Beauregard is enjoying himself and you can hear his deep baying receding as he chases, or is chased by, a rabbit or squirrel. Or alligator?

What seems like hours go by before the dog comes back, soaking wet and filthy dirty but wagging his tail and wearing what you're sure is a wide grin. With a superhuman effort you get him into the dinghy and peer through the dark looking for the anchor light. There it is, dead to windward, so you start rowing. When it seems as though your arms will come out of their sockets with one more pull, you run into the hull of your boat, fall over backward onto the dog, and, accompanied by anguished screams of pain from Beauregard and accusations of cruelty from your wife, you risk permanent disability by lifting him onto the deck. Somehow you climb aboard, go below, and get your foul-weather gear off just as you collapse into your bunk.

As your head hits the pillow you hear your wife whisper, "Honey, are you awake? Did you make sure Beauregard did everything he was supposed to do?" And that's when you resolve that either Beauregard goes or you go. And at that moment you really don't care which.

The story I have just told may seem farfetched, but it happens to every dog-owning seaman sooner or later. Even if you feed your pet a new Science Diet that leaves little residue, it doesn't take a lot of residue to spoil new carpeting. And if your dog doesn't get the kind of food it has grown accustomed to eating, the problem can be a lot more serious. Some owners swear by the new soft-moist foods which make our dog sick. Of course, that type of food means that you must give your dog a lot of water, creating another problem. The end result remains the same: you've got to row ashore several times a day. Either that or you train the dog to use some area on the deck to relieve itself.

Most of us like to cruise in sunny climates. Dogs are subject to sunstroke. That means you have to keep your dog in a shady spot at all times. You could use your own body to shade the dog in an emergency, ignoring the fact that you may suffer from the same problem in doing so. But avid dog lovers brush such objections aside, saying anything is worth the trouble if you love your dog. And that's my point. It's difficult to continue to love your dog when it becomes a pain in the neck to you. Most people have their dogs before they buy their boats. By the time they discover that dogs on boats can be a problem, they love the animals too much to give them to friends to care for during their absence. Their excuse is that the dog is unhappy when it's with strangers. How do they know? It's quite possible the pet would heave a sigh of relief to get back on good old *terra firma.* The next time you see a dog being carried up a ladder, paws dug into its owner's back, and trembling violently from fear, see if you can detect a happy smile on its face.

"But what about the protection you get with a dog aboard?" That's a question many will ask. Unless you have a Doberman pinscher trained to kill, no dog can discourage a determined thief. And how do you train a dog to distinguish between well-dressed thieves and poorly dressed friends or relatives? Big dogs tend to be gentle and a pat on the head from a total stranger will lull the dog into thinking it has found a new friend. Small dogs are more protective and far noisier, but what self-respecting pilferer will be scared off by a yipping poodle? Beauregard could sleep through a complete ransacking of the boat, even to the point of being lifted off a hatch for easier entry. No, protection is better achieved with an electronic device or by leaving someone aboard when in a strange port.

People claim that having a dog aboard does not present a problem of fleas or hair. Baloney! What actually happens is that cruising dog owners get accustomed to having fleas aboard and learn to adjust to having stray hairs over much of the boat. According to these people, fleas climb on the dog when the animal is ashore but they get off as the dog gets aboard the boat. I've also noticed that these same people seem to scratch a lot while they're telling you their stories. Eventually, the question is whether the dog's fleas are getting onto the people or the other way around.

I once read an article describing the joys of cruising with a dog aboard. The subject of exercise for the dog was described as being a joyful experience. Take the dog along while you shop. You know how welcome a dog is in a grocery store. Particularly a dog that is trained to attack strangers. Leaving the dog tied outside invites lawsuits from parents whose children have been devoured or dismembered. If you take the dog for a walk while your clothes are in the laundromat, you risk losing your clothes. And the thought of throwing a stick for my dog on the beach, after having sailed for ten hours against a stiff chop, doesn't do much for me. I like to set the hook, flake out in the cockpit, and have my wife serve me a long, cooling drink. The answer would be to train the dog to jump into the water, swim to shore, run around madly for an hour, swim back to the boat, and then climb the ladder by itself. If it could learn to go up to the bow and shake itself off, so much the better. That's not asking too much of man's best friend, is it?

Finally, the fun of cruising is meeting friends and enjoying an afternoon or evening aboard their boats, laughing and drinking, and exchanging sea stories. Nothing can dampen the party like having your wife break into your favorite tale of heroism at sea with a reminder that it's time to take the dog ashore for you-know-what. No, my friends, boats and dogs do not make a happy combination. As I've told my wife on numerous occasions, if God had meant for dogs to sail, He'd have given them masts and rudders instead of legs and a tail.

I had something else I wanted to say but my wife just reminded me it's time to take Beauregard ashore. "Yes, dear. I'll make sure he does everything."

Don't Mess Around with Mother Nature

⚓ *NOVEMBER, 1978*

"Whether he's right or whether he's not, we're going to have forecasts, weather or not."

OK, so that isn't the way it goes, but it's close enough to get the message across. The point I want to make is that we boat owners are getting short-changed by the National Weather Service and the National Oceanic and Atmospheric Administration (NOAA). When you consider how much tax money goes into satellites that beam photos back to earth, weather stations and buoys, weather broadcasts that

prove fiction isn't dead, and weather predictions that have to be products of a warped sense of humor, you have to admit that something's
wrong. Too many of us have been caught out in bad weather, despite
assurances from forecasters that it's a great day for a family picnic.

Let me give you a case in point. This column is being written on
the bridge of my Huckins cruiser as we run the hundred miles from
Green Turtle Cay in the Abacos to West End on Grand Bahama Island. As we upped anchor this morning, the weather forecasts called
for four days of perfect weather, with an occasional shower in the
area. Three hours out, I looked up to see the biggest, blackest, most
threatening sky I've ever seen heading my way. Lightning was flashing
enough to make me worry about hanging on to the wheel.

Suddenly, we were plunged into a 60-knot rain squall that
blocked out all visibility. At the moment, the sky has returned to a dull
gray and the rain has slowed to a drizzle. Now to find West End channel before the next squall hits—I can see one making up now.

If this was the first time I'd been led up the garden path by a
weather forecaster, I'd say OK—he's entitled to one mistake. But because it happens all the time, I must ask if I'm not entitled to an occasional correct forecast. As it is, I have to resort to some old, faithful
methods, like letting my bursitis warn me about changes for the worse.
The only problem is that the older I get, the more frequently my bursitis is the result of lifting too many glasses of rum punch.

For a while, I even tried "Red sky in the morning, sailor's warning; red sky at night, sailor's delight." That turned out to be as bad as
the National Weather Service, and I suspect they use it for guidance.

No, fellow skippers, there have got to be some changes made, and
I've a few thoughts on the subject. As if you didn't know.

How about installing Weather Watchers in low-flying satellites,
like those guys in helicopters who tell us how bad traffic is? These
Weathernauts would be selected on their records. Those having the
lowest accuracy percentages would be picked first. If their accuracy
remained low, NOAA would enforce conjugal visits, while the man
with the best average each month would be protected from his old
lady.

If that seems too costly, we might try a different tack. Suppose we
turn weather forecasting over to women? What could be more natural
than a woman analyzing the thought processes of the lady who dic-
tates our weather, Mother Nature?

My wife is a perfect example of a woman who can analyze another gal's motives at first glance. Whenever some cute thing with lots of curves and long legs appears, my wife will whisper, "Don't stare at her. She's a hussy." Without my wife, I'd never have known that all busty young women are either tramps or hussies.

Or take when I'd hire a secretary and my wife would ask right away, "How many words a minute does she type?" I'd have to admit that with her figure, it was doubtful she could see the keyboard. Eventually, I'd have to fire her because it would turn out that she couldn't type at all. My wife eventually took over the hiring herself, and I found that life was a lot less exciting . . . but safer.

Now the same thing could happen if we had a gal at the head of the National Weather Service. Life would be safer. Duller, but safer, and on a small boat in open water, that ain't all bad.

Finally, I offer what is really the best, most logical solution to the problem. Everyone (with the exception of a few crazed women's libbers) knows that men are more solid and predictable and of sounder judgment than are women. Therefore, it seems only common sense to wrest weather control away from *Mother* Nature, and put it in the hands of *Father* Nature.

With a man at the helm, storms would stay on track, hurricanes would blow straight out to sea, rain would fall only on Monday through Friday, and water spouts would be repelled by boats. Now, that's *my* kind of weather—manly weather. Straightforward, logical, well organized. Why even the National Weather Service might be able to predict it.

Let's Hear It for Natural Gas!

⚓ *DECEMBER, 1978*

If I told you that you're sitting on a mother lode of cheap, unlimited, and readily available energy, you'd pooh-pooh the whole idea. Yet it's true that you have within you the solution to the world's energy shortage. It's called methane gas, and it's formed by the decomposition of "epa" (in honor of the folks who brought us MSDs). Unfortunately, the

EPA-crats are destroying this source, forcing us to macerate it, aerate it, separate it, and colorate it until it isn't worth a bean.

This is an outrage considering the advantages of methane power. It's easy to generate—just leave a holding tank to bake in the noonday sun. And it requires no regulation, except in crowded elevators. All that is required to achieve a state of total independence from the Arabs is to put a stop to the EPA's disastrous efforts to control the sanitary conditions in, on, and around our boats.

What the EPA should do is supply each boat owner with a tiny converter that would change supplies of epa into power for lighting, cooking, propulsion, and heating. After all, the government is subsidizing a Florida dairy farmer to the tune of a million dollars to perfect his system for turning cow flops into methane gas. What I want to know is, what makes cow epa better than people epa? If this guy's idea works, we'll just be kowtowing to dairy farmers instead of Arabs. Considering the price of milk and cheese, we'd be better off with the Arabs.

If one cow can produce enough methane to power a city of twelve thousand people, it stands to reason that a family of four could produce enough to power a fifty-two-foot twin-screw cruiser on a circumnavigation at 17 knots. A family of eight heavy eaters could keep an eighty-footer in gas, as long as their appetites held out.

The possibilities are endless, but first we must wrest control from those power-mad beaureaucrats in Washington. Then we have to change the attitude of people to epa. In other words, what's needed is a new program of toilet training for adults. Overeating would be encouraged. Starchy foods would be sold at a discount, with special subsidies to bean farmers. Mothers would command children, "Eat already, so we can take the boat out for a spin." Chicago wouldn't be the only "Windy City." What is now considered a faux pas would become a bravura performance.

If all this seems overblown, consider the alternative. With a single stroke of the pen, some yo-yo in Washington has decreed that your expensive boat will become a floating outhouse at worst, or a floating sewage plant at best. A crowded anchorage over the Fourth of July will be unbearable, if not downright dangerous. Holding tanks have been known to explode with considerable force, after all, accounting for the occasional blue body you see careening through the air.

Even if you're fortunate enough to escape an explosion, you still have the nightmare of disposing of blue epa. Nobody wants it. Can you blame them?

But just think what will happen when all of us say, "No more! Enough! We reject holding tanks, macerators, flow-through MSDs, and all the other insanities EPA has dreamed up. We demand miniature converters that can be easily fitted on boats. We demand that you subsidize epa conversion, and stop destroying the most natural gas of all!"

It's either that, or a return to the good old days of the wooden bucket. Don't laugh. There are designers working this very moment on yachts with no heads as we know them today. Instead of a cubbyhole stuck down in the bowels of the vessel, there will be a boomkin projecting off the stern with a plain and simple seat. Sports fishermen will have rodholders affixed to their thrones, a terrific advantage when fighting a marlin for hours on end. On a rough day, this device will have all the advantages of both a head and a bidet, while providing invigorating fresh air and an inspiring view.

It simply proves that those old naval architects knew what they were doing when every vessel had a poop deck. And it holds out hope that someday, we won't have MSDs or even an EPA. That, fellow yachtsmen, is the straight poop.

Can't They Leave Us Alone?

⚓ *OCTOBER, 1977*

I've been waiting all summer long to go cruising in the Bahamas, but now that the weather has cooled down enough to venture out of the air-conditioning, I'm afraid to leave the dock.

I'm not worried about the Gulf Stream or the Bahamian reefs or making it to Man-O'-War Cay. I'm worried about what little tricks our government has in store while I'm gone. Everything keeps changing as government agencies scramble around for something to do. You can go out for a day of fishing secure in the knowledge that you are legal, then return a few hours later to discover things have changed and you face twenty years in prison.

Take radiotelephones. I recently bought a boat that had a beautiful double-sideband radio aboard. Now it's useless unless I'm in dire straits. So I'm compelled to use my VHF, which doesn't cover enough distance to let me get too far offshore. My VHF set came with six channels, including the wrong weather channel for my area and the wrong crystal for the marine operator. On top of that, the Coast Guard comes on channel 16 and tells everybody to listen for important news to be broadcast on channel 22, which I don't have. But I hesitate to buy the crystals because by the time they're installed they'll be obsolete.

Single sideband is just as bad, if not worse. A friend of mine recently bought a new SSB at considerable cost. Then he read where the Federal Communications Commission (FCC) is planning to change all the frequencies and that means he has to buy new crystals. And they're not cheap. It certainly sounds like a plot, but it's tough trying to finger the guilty parties.

Then there's the change to meters from the normal American system that has served us well for two hundred years or so. Now we're being asked to think in different terms. Can you imagine what that's going to do to boat owners? If nautical miles per hour are called "knots," what will they call nautical meters per hour? Kneats? Meats? Knuts!

Can you see yourself navigating in the thin waters of the Bahamas or Chesapeake and your fathometer is indicating in meters? By the time you convert from meters to feet, you're hard aground. Then you call the Coast Guard on your illegal, obsolete AM radiotelephone and explain to them why you're using an illegal set, even if it is an emergency. Then you try to give them a location in meters, only to discover the Coast Guard hasn't been told about the change, or their equipment won't measure in meters. Finally, you spend an hour describing your boat in meters, and the height of your crew members in meters, and by then the tide has turned and you float off.

If you own a Loran-A set, you're faced with tossing it overboard because the Coast Guard, or somebody, has decided that A is *not* good but C *is* good. Or you can buy an A set now and have it converted to C at some future date, or buy a C set and wait for a while until there are enough C stations. It's enough to drive you over the edge of the world, which Columbus worried about even before the days when the government developed its well-known interferiority complex.

And of course there are the "head" regulations. These tell the world what kind of mentality we have running the show in Washington. With every waterfront town pouring millions of gallons of raw sewage into our rivers and lakes every day, boat owners are being required to rebuild and replumb their boats to accommodate some goofy system that won't work worth a hoot, won't benefit the ecology, and won't do anything for anybody but the manufacturers of equipment.

Last year I bought a twenty-three-channel CB so that I could talk to my friends in the marina without having to leave my air-conditioning and gin and tonic. Now, most of my friends have forty-channel CBs and are too busy using their other channels to listen to me anymore. But I'll fix them. I'm buying one of the new SSB CBs, which has greater range (and is, of course, incompatible with the old CBs) so I can talk to the boys at the next marina.

Then there are the new International Rules of the Road. Just as I was beginning to get the old rules down pat, there are new ones to learn. First, the international rules applied beyond major headlands. Then one morning I woke up to discover that the imaginary line had moved to my doorstep—wherever that is. Since all of the chart numbers have changed, I can't even figure out what new chart to order to get away from it all.

Them

⚓ *FEBRUARY, 1979*

When I told my friends in California that Dory and I were moving to Florida, they warned me about mosquitoes, no-see-ums, and cockroaches. Nobody mentioned palmetto bugs.

During the nine years we've lived on the East Coast, we have seldom been bothered by mosquitoes, have yet to see a Florida cock-

Nobody mentioned the palmetto bugs.

roach, and only rarely suffered those little red welts left by no-see-ums. But we're experts on palmetto bugs.

There are those who say that palmetto bugs are nothing more than giant cockroaches. Not so. My daughter, Barbara, lives in an expensive New York apartment furnished with honest-to-goodness cockroaches. They are small, fast, smart and elusive. Palmetto bugs are huge, lumbering, not overly bright, and have great difficulty eluding a determined hunter armed with a can of insecticide and a long-handled mallet.

The problem with palmetto bugs is that they fly. This means that watching TV on a warm evening is sure to attract a few who enter through an open window. On our boat there is never any doubt when a palmetto bug visits because my wife lets out a scream, I race to the galley for the bug bomb, and she hops up on the coffee table to keep the p.b. at bay with a rolled-up newspaper. Then follows a period of: SCREAM . . . POINT . . . SPRAY . . . SMASH . . . as I follow the little bugger around the furniture in an effort to corner him and administer the coup de grâce.

I've said that palmetto bugs aren't as smart as the northern German cockroaches, but that doesn't mean they're stupid. For example, they never fly through the window during a commercial. No, they arrive when there are fifty seconds left in the Monday night football game and the losing quarterback has just unleashed a forty-yard desperation pass to his wide receiver.

Another indication of their intelligence is their behavior when discovered. Palmetto bugs are night creatures. They love to forage for food in the galley when the lights are out. When you flick on the lights, they don't scamper for cover. They freeze. Not until you make a move do they make theirs. So the trick is to sneak into the galley, armed with spray and mallet, then flick on the light while poised for the kill. Always spray first because this tends to slow down their reflexes and makes the terrain slippery. Follow with a well-armed blow, hopefully when the creature is planted on something unbreakable and not your new chronograph.

It is important to make certain you've finished him off. (You don't want to face a bruised and vindictive p.b. in the morning.) Palmetto bugs are similar to the sturdy todos santos flies of Ensenada, Mexico, and the marsh flies of South Carolina and Georgia in that they have this peculiar ability to withstand punishment. I've found it takes three hard blows with the mallet or a rolled-up edition of the Sunday *New*

York Times to do them in. The first blow gets their attention, the second slows them down, and the third smashes them into total deadness (R. I. Palmetto). Even then I pick up the remains with a paper towel and toss them overboard.

My old friend Fritz Seyfarth has long advocated crickets as a deterrent to cockroaches. I don't disagree, but I doubt that a cricket is capable of handling a fully grown palmetto bug. In fact, I've heard of crickets being found in a state of dismemberment near a known palmetto bug hangout.

Others contend that lizards kill palmetto bugs. But I discovered two huge p.b.s carrying off a medium-sized lizard to what I assumed would be a barbecue.

To date, the only solution (outside of mallets) we have discovered is a small box of poison called "Roach Motel." These contain food palmetto bugs love plus an ingredient that will eventually do them in. Another deterrent is a kitten. Cats love to catch palmetto bugs and beat the hell out of them. If you can keep the cat from dipping into the Roach Motel, you could win the battle.

For those of you who say, "You only find bugs in a dirty kitchen," let me assure you of one more thing: a palmetto bug can live for four days on the grease from a fingerprint. Hand me my mallet.

"Pardon Me, boy, Is This the Chattanooga Poo-Poo?
⚓ *JANUARY, 1980*

Since our government has chosen to turn our yachts into floating outhouses, it seems appropriate to mention a situation that points out how stupid the government's head law really is. Among the many operations the bureaucracy mismanages these days is Amtrak. You remember Amtrak. That's the railroad system the government has decided to cut back on now that the public is starting to use it. Well, I had occasion to ride Amtrak not long ago and discovered that Amtrak is breaking the law. That is, if you assume that what applies to one segment of the population should apply to all other segments. I'm referring to the law that requires boat owners to install holding tanks or expensive treatment plants aboard their boats while allowing train riders to deposit toilet contents directly on the track bed below.

You recall the old song, "Passengers will please refrain from flushing toilets while the train is standing in the station, I love you." Well, the same signs are on display in today's trains because there's a direct shot from toilet bowl to ground below on Amtrak. Considering that Amtrak recently boasted of carrying several million passengers over a short period of time, it follows that several million deposits must have been made directly onto the ground wherever Amtrak travels.

Under normal logic, this would be a direct contradiction. But when the Environmental Protection Agency (EPA) and government bureaucracy are concerned, logic seldom rears its head. So, while some three million boat owners will be forced to install costly sewage plants in their boats to prevent *caca* from going into the water, some three million other citizens will be allowed to leave their droppings wherever Amtrak's tracks are laid, including railroad crossings in the middle of town, and bridges that pass over otherwise virgin springs and streams.

How could such stupidity prevail, you might well ask. Well, if you consider that the primary purpose of the EPA is to make certain that it expands its control so as to create more income and prestige for its members, you begin to understand. If you add to that the lively lobbying which the toilet manufacturers were guilty of during the hearing period, you begin to put two and two together and come up with the conclusion that a handful of greedy and misguided dodos has passed laws that will benefit no one but themselves. Was it ever any different?

Personally, I think the three million boat owners who are being forced to comply with the new head regulations should file a class action suit against the EPA to determine whose idea it was in the first place, who stands to gain the most, and why any boat owner should obey a law that is unfair, discriminatory, stupid, inflationary, and typical of government's ever-encroaching interference in the lives of common citizens. But boat owners are not joiners. They aren't organized. Boat owners generally buy boats to get away from the land-based confusion and conformity that is driving us all crazy. So, assuming we'll never get organized, what is the next best step?

Well, the EPA has said we can't deposit *caca* in the water but it is okay for people to deposit it on railroad tracks or roadbeds. The obvious answer then is for all of us to follow the lead of Amtrak. I suggest we empty our holding tanks on railroad tracks, if possible. Should such tracks not be convenient when emptying time arrives, do the next best thing—use the street in front of the marina.

Don't tell me it isn't legal! If it's legal for Amtrak to dump it on the ground, then it's legal for boat owners to do the same thing. The health hazard is no greater on the street than it is on the roadbed. And what's good for the Amtrak rider is good for the boat owner.

If that doesn't appeal to you, how about sending your contents to the EPA by UPS via a biodegradable trash bag? Three million bags of you-know-what stacked up in the EPA's executive offices should get somebody's attention. We don't expect to get favorable action by such a method. That would be asking too much. After all, the EPA has to show the country how tough it is. Particularly since giant corporations are pouring billions of gallons of poisons into rivers, lakes, and waterways every month without receiving more than a tap on the wrist. The boat owners are easy game because they're all rich and can afford to spend five hundred to a thousand dollars for a useless gadget that doesn't really work to begin with.

What can you lose by standing up for your rights? Well, there's the fines and warnings handed out by the Coast Guard, the already overworked service that hasn't time these days to guard much coast, what with all of the extra duties being dumped in its lap. I suppose a few unlucky souls will ultimately be handed stiff fines and the rest of the boating community will fall in line to avoid having to pour good money after bad. But it doesn't have to be that way.

I suggest that when the Coast Guard is forced to implement this stupid regulation, in between saving lives and catching dope smugglers, then the accused parties be given the same courtesy as Senator Herman Talmadge received in his recent embarrassment. You will recall that old Herm got caught cheating and lying and doing what every politician is expected to do in the execution of his duties. Well, if *you* had done what Herm did, you'd be staring out through prison bars about now, looking forward to visitors' day. But the Senate has a system that would work just fine for boat owners accused of bypassing the new head regulation.

First, you'd be hauled before a gathering of your peers for judgment. In this case it would be a group of boat owners who had also refused to conform to the law. Somebody would get up and denounce you and somebody else would then respond with stories of how well you treat your family and list your civic contributions. Then all present would look very grave and finally you'd be chastised by having your actions called reprehensible. Don't be alarmed. It isn't nearly as bad as you might think, particularly since the Senate has altered the meaning of the word. By their definition, "reprehensible" means "naughty."

So, having been labeled reprehensible by your peers, you would emerge from court wearing a slack-mouthed grin and declare a victory. Then your peers would pat you on the back and heave mighty sighs of relief that they hadn't been caught being naughty. Subsequently, everybody would go back to their boats, flush their heads, and say to themselves, "There, but for the luck of the Irish, go I."

Whichever way you look at it, the whole thing stinks.

The Liedtke Syndrome

⚓ *DECEMBER, 1979*

When I was a young lad, I can recall signs hanging over the back bars of Chicago's saloons that read "WATSMMHATTAH."

The literal translation was, "Why Are There So Many More Horse's Asses Than There Are Horses?"

I thought of this a few weeks ago when I stumbled across a news item in the *New York Times* that told of one Klaus Liedtke, described as being the acting director of the Weather Modification Office of the National Oceanic and Atmospheric Administration in Boulder, Colorado.

It seems that in May of 1978, five aircraft were fitted with special equipment that would allow them to seed budding hurricanes with silver iodide and thus dissipate their high winds. After Hurricane David had managed to kill thousands of people, leave millions homeless, and destroy dreams and families in such poverty-ridden areas as Dominica, Haiti, and the Dominican Republic, some reporter thought it might be interesting to know why Acting Director Liedtke had not acted to save some of these unfortunate people from the misery left by the storm.

"Our aircraft were in an experiment in the Indian Ocean, out of Diego Garcia, and they arrived back here fairly late. A decision was made not to attempt a seeding this year," said Mr. Liedtke.

I suppose it would be out of line to question the government as to why planes slated to seed Atlantic hurricanes are based in Colorado, inasmuch as this makes as much sense as any other decision the government makes these days. After all, you wouldn't want these planes to be near the National Hurricane Center in Miami. Everybody knows that hurricanes originate in Colorado, right? If Mr. Liedtke was situated in Florida, where he might have lost everything he held dear when Hurricane David threatened to come ashore, you can bet your bippie those planes would have been out there dumping silver iodide like it was going out of style.

I'll tell you something. While I was running for cover up the New River in Fort Lauderdale, I thought about the hurricane-seeding program (which languished during the Nixon administration) and wondered what had happened to it. If someone had told me NOAA could have reduced David's power by 20 percent just by a bit of seeding, I'd have been on the phone yelling, "Seed! Seed, for God's sake!" And so would every other resident of the Caribbean and the Gulf Coast, as well as the entire East Coast.

Now, you'd think with so many millions of people being threatened by hurricanes that Mr. Liedtke would have noticed that people were dying while he was trying to come to a decision. I mean, even if his planes had only saved a few hundred lives, and only ten or twenty millions of dollars in property, it would seem to me it would be worth the trip. That is why our tax dollars were used to equip and man the planes, isn't it? It is why our tax dollars pay Mr. Liedtke's salary, isn't it? Or have I missed the point somehow?

I don't suppose the thousands who were injured or lost their homes can look to Mr. Liedtke for recompense, but surely they can look to him for a better explanation than "our planes were in an experiment in the Indian Ocean." Why were our planes in the Indian Ocean during hurricane season in the Atlantic? Why weren't the planes flown back to the States at the first sign that David was a major hurricane? If they got back too late for David, couldn't they have seeded Frederick?

Well, I suppose we'll never know. But one thing really bothers me. I expect to be in Florida next year during hurricane season. It would be of some comfort to know that should another killer storm brew up in the Atlantic, that the Weather Modification Office would get off its butt and start modifying. But, unfortunately, the future looks no brighter than the past. When asked about his plans for next year, Mr. Liedtke said, "No decision has been made yet." How does that grab you, hurricane watchers of the world?

I don't know what the experiment was all about in the Indian Ocean. Perhaps it had to do with getting as far away from a hurricane as possible without flying to the moon. Perhaps the folks in Diego Garcia have pull with Washington that we know nothing about. If so, let their taxes fund Mr. Liedtke and his missing planes. Meanwhile, I suggest that the seeding planes be kept closer to the hurricane breeding grounds. I suggest that Mr. Liedtke be put to sea in a small boat in the midst of the next killer storm so he can have a firsthand look at the thing. I'm sure it will appear different from that vantage point than from a satellite photo shown on the *Today* show the day after it wipes out an entire island . . . or maybe the East Coast of the United States.

Meanwhile, I'd like to nominate Klaus Liedtke for the 1979 WATSMMHATTAH Award in memory of those who, for the lack of seed, will remember David and Frederick for the rest of their lives.

No, I don't think naming the next hurricane Klaus would be appropriate.

Project Bunglegoof

⚓ *JUNE, 1980*

Normally, I'm a sweet-tempered, kindly sort of person with only the cheeriest words for my fellowman. Normally. But some things annoy me. Like government bureaucratic arrogance and stupidity. But then, everybody gets annoyed with the bureaucracy. It's just there, like a huge blob that is destined to overrun all of us someday, smothering normal human beings and taxpayers under its massive weight, and strangling those who struggle with its red tape.

So, I suppose it is only natural for a curmudgeon to respond to a response to a question I had some months ago (December 1979) about the part of the bureaucracy that deals with seeding hurricanes. As I recall, I questioned the arrogance of a man named Liedtke in answering the questions of a *New York Times* reporter. Mr. Liedtke's attitude seemed to me to reflect a complete and total disregard for the public and the press. It appeared to me to be the attitude of someone who felt he was above question. Inasmuch as several billions of dollars of damage had just been wrought by two devastating hurricanes, I thought it was in order to question where our hurricane-seeding planes might have been.

So, in my own sweet and gentle way, I wrote a column on the subject, never suspecting for a moment that I would generate reaction or response from Mr. Liedtke. But, lo and behold, there appeared a letter from a Mr. Rosenthal, who apparently runs the operation out of Miami, taking me to task for having the audacity to question the viability or necessity for the program.

"Project Stormfury," as the seeding program is called in typical government super-hype, has yet to result in a proven technology. For those of you not familiar with governmentese, what Mr. Rosenthal is trying to say is, "It doesn't work." He then goes on to point out that they couldn't find any hurricanes of the proper structure during

1977 and 1978. Adding those years to 1979 made it three strikes in a row. Under most circumstances, Mr. Rosenthal and his cohorts would be out. But this is governmental spending we are talking about and programs never die, they just hide away in hopes of being forgotten.

Mr. Rosenthal accused me of performing a disservice by distorting the facts. As I recall my column, I didn't have any facts to distort . . . and that's what prompted my questions in the first place. I didn't lead gullible readers to assume there were proven technologies. All I asked was, "If the seeding doesn't work, why spend tax dollars supporting the program? If it does work, why not use it?" Now, that doesn't sound unreasonable to me. I mean, either we are wasting money or we aren't. Is it a sin to question the government these days? Did I miss something along the way? Or are my tax dollars paying Mr. Rosenthal's salary and all those other salaries just as they have for many years now.

I'm sort of sorry I mentioned the incident, now that Rosie has risen up and defended himself so vehemently. It is probably downright embarrassing to have to justify your existence when there is so little to work with. And the flap I created within the division must have been tremendous. Poor Liedtke, trying to take the official government position that what the public doesn't know won't hurt the government. Can you imagine the chewing out he must have gotten from Rosenthal? I can just picture the conversation.

"Liedtke? Is this you, Klaus? What in hell did you say to that reporter?"

"I said nothing, sir. Just as you instructed me."

"You said too much, Dummkopf. You made that reporter mad and he reported it in the *New York Times.* Then some troublemaker who writes for Hearst picked it up and now the entire government is down on me. Thank God I was able to come up with a brilliant response. Did you read it?"

"I read it, yes, sir. But I don't understand it."

"Idiot, that's why it was brilliant. You're not supposed to understand it. I used governmentese, a language developed by the government to keep the citizenry in the dark and the bureaucracy growing."

"Whatever you say, sir. But just between you and me, I'm going to stay in my bunker until the war is over. And I would advise you to do the same. Maybe people will forget about us while we hold on until our pensions come due."

Who knows, maybe that isn't the way it was. But it wouldn't surprise me if a conversation similar to that had taken place.

What interested me was a comment that Rosenthal made at the end of his spirited defense. He questioned why I didn't ask the Surgeon General to end cancer immediately. That intrigued me. Apparently, Mr. Rosenthal puts himself on the same level as the Surgeon General and compares seeding hurricanes with fighting cancer. That really made me stop and think. Then it occurred to me that if the Surgeon General operated on the same basis that Rosenthal did, people would be smoking more cigarettes than ever while he waited for a perfectly structured cancer to appear that could be used as a test case.

Nobody could say that the Surgeon General has cured cancer, but at least he is trying. And this is the difference between the Surgeon General and Mr. Rosenthal.

Or, to put it in even simpler terms, if Mr. Rosenthal and his fellow Stormfury cohorts had been representing the United States in the Olympic hockey competition, they'd still be waiting for the ice to harden while they sharpened their skates.

I don't know what it takes to form a perfect hurricane for Mr. Rosenthal, but I hope I'm not around when it hits. In fact, knowing how he thinks on the subject, I think I'll flee to Boulder, Colorado, at the first sign that a storm is heading toward Florida.

I just hope he doesn't lock the door behind him as he goes into the headquarters. I'd hate to think I was going to die just because he was the type who carried a grudge.

For Whom Ma Bell Tolls

⚓ *DECEMBER, 1977*

Hello, the voice of experience here. Listen, next time a woman with a tenor like a B-1 bomber calls and threatens to cut off your phone service, do what I did long ago. Tear the phone out of the wall and send it to her, UPS, collect. Then fire your employees, announce that you're available as a consultant, buy a boat, and move on board. Forever.

That phone booth became my office.

The difficult part, of course, is remembering to tell yourself over and over from that day forward, "Money isn't everything." And ignoring your wife when she says, "No, it's the *only* thing."

Looking back on it, the way I got on a boat is a little bizarre, like flying to New York from London via Rangoon. Understand, I dearly love living on a boat. It's how I got here that irks me. I mean, when you consider that a simple plastic-coated speaking device can drive a grown man from his profitable career in advertising and send him skulking to sea, you begin to understand that technology has us in a half-nelson.

Anyway, when Ma Bell struck at me one day, I retaliated by closing my office and becoming a seagoing consultant. A consultant, incidentally, is a fellow who is unemployed but can't bring himself to collect unemployment insurance. To bolster my standing as a member of the gainfully semi-employed, I made one fatal error. I had a phone installed on my boat. Which is a little like asking your mugger to tea.

You guessed it. I became a phone junkie. I ran up staggering bills every month, glibly dialing California, Indiana, Maine, Paraguay. My wife grew uneasy. She kept asking me how come I had such a big phone bill and such a small income.

Years passed. Uneventfully. Unprofitably. Then, this year I pulled into my regular slip in West Palm Beach and immediately called Ma Bell about hooking up my phone as usual. I talked to a fellow who used to skin fleas for their hide and tallow, and he informed me that it would cost $117 to run a cord from a post on the dock to my boat, a distance about the length of a first down.

I explained in a gentlemanly tone that I'd already paid to have the phone jack installed on the post, and that I had my phone and extension for the past five years and simply wanted their minimum service—which is all you get anyway. The conversation ended with me banging down the receiver and attempting to dump the whole phone booth in the drink. It took three strong men and a power winch to stop me, and good thing that they did.

That phone booth became my office, and though it gets a bit cramped when I move in my desk, Bigelow carpet, and stenographer, other advantages outweigh the discomforts. For example, everybody on the dock uses this booth to receive messages. At the first ring, half a dozen people rush to pick up the phone. This gives me the most reliable answering service I've ever had. Retired bank presidents take messages for me in cultured tones, which beats the hell out of having some old hag with oversized adenoids telling clients, "Naw, I dunno where he's at."

There are other advantages. Nobody can call me collect, but I *have* to call them collect. When some unwanted caller leaves a message, I simply claim I never got it. And when I have a siege of no income, I never have to worry about the phone being shut off.

If you're trying to close a deal, one of the most frustrating things that can happen is to have your prospect say, "We'll call you in a few days." You can sit for *weeks* sweating out that remark. But the phone-booth method saves you all that anguish. You simply reply, "No, I'll call you day after tomorrow." After all, in your delicate booth-bound condition, what could be more reasonable?

Small wonder the phone booth is so popular among the numerous seagoing consultants on my dock. On a busy day, the booth is like a Paris *pissoir* next to a beer stand. A constant stream of men go in and out carrying notes and wearing "business" expressions. Each man understands the importance of not tying up the "convenience" too long and acts accordingly.

Like me, they've discovered that an office works as well on Pier 6 as at 666 Madison, all thanks to the marvels of the modern phone booth. And if we go in like mild-mannered Clark Kents, we emerge—business done—as Superboatmen. Ready to lift tall gin and tonics on the bridge deck faster than a speeding Cigarette.

Hold all calls!

Blackbeard Was a Piker!

⚓ *FEBRUARY, 1978*

Do you get the feeling you're being shafted each time you sign a check for your marine insurance premium? Or pay a yard bill? Don't worry about being paranoid, because you probably *are* being shafted . . . and by experts. In fact, shafting is frequently their only area of expertise. Who's doing all the shafting? A lot of people, my friend, but not necessarily the insurance company. In fact, you and your insurance company are usually co-victims of the latter-day boatyard buccaneers, those wily predators who claim more victims each year than the Bermuda Triangle, the Great White Shark, and Blackbeard combined.

If you doubt my word, talk to a dozen boat owners and you'll hear a dozen horror stories told by normally mild-mannered yachtsmen who've been transformed into raging maniacs as they watched incompetent boatyard mechanics muddle through a repair job at the speed of an arthritic snail. I speak from firsthand knowledge, having recently spent six weeks in a famous old boatyard. There I watched a team of Portuguese-speaking machinists struggle to fathom the mystery of repairing underwater gear I'd wiped out when I hit some rocks.

At first I thought the people who ran the yard had a grudge against me. But I soon discovered that they treated everyone badly. A small comfort, I'll admit, but better than thinking I'd been singled out for special consideration. In retrospect, I can see where I made some basic errors in judgment. The first, of course, was leaving the wrong lighthouse on the wrong side at a speed of 16 knots. The second was assuming that a yard with a "Famous Old Name" had more to offer than just the Famous Old Name. It didn't. The third error was thinking I'd receive some sympathy for my plight and some gentle, diplomatic bolstering of my morale. It was soon apparent that I was looked upon as a delivery man who had just brought next month's mortgage payment by boat . . . my boat! The closest I got to a warm greeting was a snarl from the yard superintendent, a fellow whose disposition swung from dour to sour.

I'm not saying that boatyards should provide psychiatric treatment for customers suffering from the aftershock of bad accidents. Boatyard operators have their own problems. Running a yard is a thankless business, at best. Certainly, the profits have to be minimal and the agitation level above normal. What with the government doing its best to regulate boatyards out of business as fast as possible, the cost of doing business going up daily, and the quality of work being produced by inexperienced employees going down, it's a wonder anyone bothers to run a yard. But we all know that boating attracts a strange bunch of characters who'd rather mess around in boats than make a buck. Unfortunately, it also attracts some folks who mess around in our boats for the sole purpose of making a buck.

The trick, obviously, is to find a yard owned by a guy who loves boats and who has managed to keep a bunch of talented and experienced old geezers working when their peers are in Florida, filling one of those crypts real-estate developers fondly call condominiums. Given a choice between a grouchy old goat with gnarled fingers and a potbelly, or a long-haired hippie puffing on a joint with a vacant expression on his pimply face, I'll take the old goat every time. But I was caught unawares at the Famous Old Boatyard because their men were middle-aged and terribly confused. We dubbed them "the Three Stooges" because each appeared to be working from a different script. Had I been watching them on TV, I might have thought their act was hilarious. But when I considered I was paying them twenty dollars an hour each (they only worked on our boat on Saturdays), there was little humor to be found.

A fourth error I committed was in letting the yard know my job was an insurance claim. This is like inviting the fox into the hen house. It was my first exposure to that grand old American custom of "letting the insurance company pay for it." This calls for a little favor here and a small kickback there and, presto, everybody comes out smelling like roses. Everybody except the insurance company. They pay the bill and raise the rates to compensate for this little game that "doesn't hurt anybody," and when your bill and mine reflect this practice, we bitch to high heaven about the cost of insurance. It's a lousy system that benefits the chiselers in our society and penalizes the honest and naïve. Nobody comes out smelling like a rose. They just come out smelling.

A fifth error I made was in not retaining my own surveyor. Not that the surveyor the insurance company hired was incompetent. It's just that he works for the insurance company. I needed a surveyor who was looking out for my interests. Had I done so, I'd probably have moved my boat to another nearby yard. Certainly, I'd have been successful in getting an estimate on the job. Can you believe that the Famous Old Yard refused to give me an estimate on five separate occasions, pacifying me with assurances that "the insurance company will pay for everything!" When they said "everything" they were referring to their monthly payroll, back taxes, and whatever odds and ends they could slip into the bill under the heading "miscellaneous." I finally took to putting down the hours the men put in on my work, including nosing about the machinist shop, getting quotes on shafts and props, etc. I had plenty of time to do this because we sat out of the water in the steamy polluted air of the boatyard for nearly six weeks.

At first I had difficulty in understanding why a ten-day job should be taking thirty days to accomplish. Then I realized that every step was being done twice. It was sort of a show-and-tell program, which required undoing what had just been done. My sixth error was not asking if these men had done this kind of work before. As it turned out, they hadn't. Their specialty was apparently in working with aluminum sailboats. My boat was wood sheathed in fiberglass, a form of construction apparently unknown in Portugal. I began to suspect things were going amiss when an old geezer of a foreman from another department insisted that my Three Stooges remove a shaft and strut they'd just installed (on a Saturday at time and a half) without proper alignment.

During all of this time, a strange situation developed concerning the repainting of the bottom. The yard supervisor assured me my insurance would cover the cost. My insurance company assured me it was not automatic. The yard then became annoyed because I had raised the subject with the insurance agent. I then became suspicious and gave strict orders to the paint foreman that I would not pay for the bottom job if the insurance company balked. Ultimately, the bottom was painted and the boat was put back in the water.

I hustled to the office to settle the bill, which I had estimated to be in the neighborhood of $3,500, allowing 20 percent for a bit of leeway by the yard. The account I was handed contained no justifying bills or details of the work done, just a few lines that indicated they had repaired my boat for a cost of $7,300. (Later, I discovered the insurance surveyor/adjustor had estimated the job at $4,500, but at the time I only knew that someone was being ripped off for an extra $4,000.) The most interesting part was the yard's reply to my protest.

There was no attempt to show me records or justify the charges. All they said was "Don't forget, Mr. Bradley, we worked with you on the bottom painting." Whoa there, sister, I thought. Don't include me in your little conspiracy to overcharge the insurance company. Don't infer that I was supposed to keep my mouth shut in return for a free bottom job. Particularly when the charge for the bottom painting was right there on the bill. Instead of dummying up, as the yard assumed I would do, I got on the phone to my insurance agent and said, "You're getting shafted for an extra four thousand dollars." My figures were off. They were only being shafted for three thousand dollars. But that wasn't the end of the tale.

When I first brought the boat in I told anyone who would listen that I came in on one engine. Had the Famous Old Yard sent a mechanic down to check out my other engine, he'd have discovered water in the cylinders and made minor repairs to save the engine. When we discovered, some five weeks later, that water had surged up through the exhaust system into the engine, it was too late to do anything other than rebuild it for a cost of $5,200 plus some extra yard time and hauling charges for the yard. My claim was now in the $12,500 range and I strongly anticipated a howl of protest from my agent. But such was not the case.

My insurance claim was paid in full and I was allowed to escape the clutches of the Famous Old Yard. Considering the yard had overcharged at least $3,000 for their work and that their failure to investigate my engine caused an additional $5,200 to be added to the bill, I was amazed at the insurance company's decision to pay without a protest. When I asked the surveyor how the yard could get away with this, he shrugged and said, "What can we do? If we challenge the amount, they'll simply come up with a lot of time cards and substantiating bills that we can't prove are fictitious. The only advice I can give you is to go to the yard next door if you ever need work done again."

My claim is just one of thousands the insurance company must process every year, and if they fought every one, nobody would ever get to use his boat. So, it's a rotten system. But given the American predilection for beating the system, it appears we'll have to live with what we've got.

The only advice I can offer is to keep your insurance premiums up to date, pick your boatyard on its current reputation, and keep your eyes on the buoys. And remember that a pirate doesn't necessarily wear an eye patch and carry a cutlass.

One more thing. The next time a friend describes how he and his boatyard screwed the insurance company, push him overboard.

You'll be doing all of us a favor.

FOUR

Paradise Is Where You Find It

Standing Room Only in Paradise

⚓ *MARCH, 1978*

If you've been dreaming of the day when you could drop out of the rat race, grow a beard, and sail off to some secluded anchorage, forget it. Paradise is jammed to capacity with middle-aged dropouts searching for their private place in the sun. It wasn't always that way.

Ten years ago a man who grew a beard, opted for early retirement, and announced plans to sail off in a small boat was considered to be a threat to society. Friends, relatives, and fellow workers reacted with comments that ranged from dismay to disgust. Neighbors withdrew behind closed doors, the boss made a note on the man's personnel file suggesting instability, senility, and possible temporary insanity. Today, half the men in my marina are middle-aged, bearded, obviously unemployed, and totally unashamed of their situations. It's a different world.

The dream has been replaced by reality. "Someday" has become "today." Obstacles which seemed insurmountable a few years ago are now swept aside as being irrelevant. People don't talk about dropping out; they do it. Doctors, lawyers, teachers, business executives . . . it makes no difference what a man has been doing. Each has a point beyond which he refuses to go. Unfortunately, the pressures and frustrations of life are pushing more and more successful men over the edge. The problem is simply that we've run out of room down here in paradise. But still they come, thousands of them every fall, filled with the anticipation of taking a few weeks to get organized in some plush Florida marina, then on to the islands and the "good life." Boy, do they have a surprise coming.

Remember that the men I'm talking about jumped the gun. They didn't wait until they were sixty-five and had their pensions and Social Security plus a comfortable income from investments. These fellows just got up one morning and said, "To hell with it! Let the kids work their way through college. Let the bank worry about the mortgage on the house. Let somebody else worry about the crabgrass and taxes. Let the boss find some other jerk to kick around. I don't know about you, but I'm going cruising!"

Caution is thrown to the wind and wifely doubts are overridden with supreme confidence that "something will turn up to bring in some dough. Besides, cruising is a cheap way to live." Unfortunately, nobody is around to advise him on the facts. One being that there is very little chance of something turning up to produce income. The other being the cost of cruising. Cruising can be less expensive than living a normal shoreside life. But it ain't cheap. Even if a hundred experienced liveaboarders talked to him like a Dutch uncle, he wouldn't change his mind. His attitude is, and quite rightly, "No, by God, I've made my decision and I'm going to stick with it. Stand back, because I'm coming through!"

So, he sells the house and the car, borrows on his life insurance, gets a ten-year mortgage on the boat, and comes up with enough in the bank to keep him going for three years—if he's careful. What he doesn't know is that most converts to the cruising life run out of money halfway through the trip. Don't ask me where the money goes, it just goes. Slip rents are higher than anticipated. Haul-outs cost twice what they did back home. Engines develop problems. The kids need a few bucks here and there to get them over rough spots. Eating out to celebrate each new stop takes its toll. Then, as might be expected, the day of reckoning arrives.

"You mean to tell me we're overdrawn? That's impossible. We've only been gone from home for a year and a half. What did you do with all that money? No, don't tell me. I don't want to know." What is he going to do now? It's mid-November, he's 1,500 miles from home, overdrawn at the bank, overextended on his credit cards, behind in his boat mortgage and insurance payments, and scared to death. That's right, just plain scared. Do you know what frightens him the most? The fear that he might have to go back to work . . . now. The thought of asking his old boss for his job never enters his mind. He burned too many bridges before he left to sneak back with his tail between his legs. Besides, he's determined he's going to make this thing work. All it takes is a little luck and a lot of thinking.

Somehow, he manages to stay semi-solvent. He does a little consulting or free-lancing. He becomes a yacht broker or he peddles insurance. He tries to write a book and gives up. He pressures a few former customers to pay old debts and he sells the remaining shares of stock. During the season his wife works in a department store, even though he assures her this is apt to hurt his image as a successful entrepreneur. He hangs on.

Finally, the situation eases. He finds a way to make a meager living without being held to a nine-to-five job. He learns the art of surviving. During the winter months, when slip rentals are high, he takes extended cruises in the Bahamas, where he anchors out and eats a lot of fish and conch. When he has to come back to the mainland to make a few bucks, he knows where to find a slip for a few dollars a night. He becomes browner, healthier looking, and at ease with himself and the world. Unfortunately, he's the guy who is screwing up paradise.

If he'd planned better, he'd have had three years of cruising with no problems and then gotten bored with it. Then he'd sell his boat and go back to Newark or some other garden spot and spend the rest of his life telling sea stories to his grandchildren. Instead of that, he stayed long enough to get soft in the head from the sun and accustomed to being a boat bum and now we've got him with us forever. He's the guy who's anchored in your favorite spot and he's the guy who just grabbed the last slip in your favorite low-overhead marina.

If there was just one of him, life would not be complicated. But there are thousands of him and more on the way. For all I know, you may be one of those who are planning to join the crowd in paradise. I beg of you, think carefully. Wait until you have a huge bank balance and both pension and Social Security checks coming in steadily. Don't rush into this thing without a lot of thought. You owe it to your country to stay where you are and work, at least for another ten years.

By then, I figure I'll be too old to care one way or the other.

Meantime, I want to keep what's left of paradise to myself. I know of a few great spots to drop the hook and a few marinas that haven't raised slip rents sky-high as yet. I'm resigned to the fact that the Bahamas will someday look like Catalina, with boats jammed rail to rail. That's what *Time* calls getting "Californicated."

All it takes to keep paradise from that fate is for you to keep telling yourself the time isn't right to make the move South. Just keep saying, "I like it here in the North. I like snow and slush. I like my job and my boss. I like making mortgage payments. I like . . ."

Get the picture?

Landsmanship, a Forgotten Art

⚓ *JULY, 1979*

Subscribers to marine publications are usually inundated with advice on how to kedge off a beach in Tierra del Fuego, the proper procedure to follow when your vessel has turned 180 degrees, and you're trapped in the head, and other solutions to problems you'll probably never experience, particularly if you follow some basic rules of chicken seamanship.

I have made it a point for many years to turn the page quickly when I come across a story about a disaster at sea. I can't bring myself to read about groundings, dismastings, hurricanes, waterspouts, or giant octopi waiting for me to make a slight mistake in judgment. I really don't want to know all of the terrible things that can happen when I venture away from the dock. I would rather it came as a total surprise, if it has to come at all. Meanwhile, I'll do my best to avoid getting into a position where knowing how to refasten my keel underwater would be helpful.

I happen to believe that being at sea is the only intelligent way for a man to spend his days. I don't necessarily mean drifting around from port to port. In fact, being at anchor in Man-O'-War or Green Turtle in the Bahamas will suit me nicely, thank you. Just so long as I am beyond reach of the daily newspapers and the TV screen, with the collection of gloom and doom we face every morning and night in this country. Just so long as I am surrounded by people whose principal concerns are whether the mail will arrive this week, and whether Bessie has rum raisin ice cream at the Bite Site on Man-O'-War.

When Dory and I returned to Florida last spring after six months of peace and tranquility in the Abacos, I quickly became aware of the need for a cram course in "landsmanship." I wasn't prepared for the rudeness I found in many marinas, or the pursed lips and knotted brows of the average boating person who was supposed to be having fun. But even the few days I spent in Florida prior to taking the train to New York hadn't prepared me for the trauma of arriving in the Big Apple.

The real shock comes when you walk down a New York street and notice the number of dudes wearing sneakers and carrying short-handled golf clubs. Something tells you they're not on their way to the country club for a round on the links. Nor do you get a feeling of safety when you take a subway and notice the cat across from you is cleaning his fingernails with a six-inch switchblade. These are truly the times that try men's souls. It is about then you realize that what the country needs is a Power Squadron course for yachtsmen returning from the safety of a circumnavigation in a twelve-foot ferro-cement schooner.

When you're away from our shores you're in no danger of being hit up for a donation to your most unfavorite charity, or being called for jury duty, or being audited by the IRS, or getting hit by a truck as you cross a street, or slipping in your tub and hitting your head. None of the above is apt to happen as you plug along under a bright blue sky and look down into crystal-clear waters. In fact, the most dangerous aspect of voyaging is the trip from your house to the marina by car.

The art of seamanship is never allowing yourself to get into a position where you have to know anything about the subject. My rules of seamanship are simple. I never leave on a Friday. I go to great lengths not to get caught in stormy weather. I try my best to keep a minimum of one foot of water between my keel and the bottom. I avoid areas frequented by pods of angry killer whales and giant octopi. I practice what is known as chicken seamanship, and if it doesn't suit your macho nature, so be it. I'll see you in the boatyard.

We've been back in Florida for almost eight months and I'm still having trouble understanding what it's all about here. I'm still puzzled by what I read in the magazines, and I wonder if we've all taken leave of our senses. Like last week I read that a cosmetics manufacturer had introduced a scented nail polish. For whom? Women who can raise their toes to their noses? Or how about the nationwide bakery chain that introduced a new health bread with extra fiber. It turned out that the fiber came from trees! While you thought you were eating a healthful, high-fiber bread, what you were really consuming was a soft Presto log. The FDA stopped them when it was learned consumers were being attacked by killer woodpeckers.

But perhaps the greatest benefit in cruising offshore is being able to get away from news about the goings-on in Washington. In this morning's paper, for instance, an oil industry official revealed that while diesel costs less to produce than gasoline and offers better mileage, you get less usable diesel fuel from a barrel of oil than you do gasoline. Can't you see it coming: having urged us to switch from gas to diesel, those idiots in D.C. will now encourage us to switch back to gas.

Okay, Washington, just give me enough fuel to get back to Man-O'-War. Landsmanship is too tough, even for curmudgeons like me.

The Ormolu State?

⚓ *APRIL, 1981*

If you've ever lived in California you know there is one dictum you must never break. It is called the California Commandment and it goes like this: Residents Shall Love, Honor, and Cherish the Golden State, in Life and in Death. Its purpose is to stop Californians from deserting the state and moving back from whence they came. Emigrating is the cardinal sin in California. The trespass is even more heinous if one moves to Florida. Well, many years ago Dory and I risked the ultimate—we heaped insult on injury by publicly declaring that we were moving from southern California to Florida because of the weather.

Californians are very defensive about their state. They refuse to acknowledge any shortcomings. I've seen dedicated Californians stand there, smoggy tears running down their cheeks, almost obscured by dense fog, hanging on to a door frame during a trembler, and assure me there is no place on earth quite so wonderful as southern California. I've sat on my boat at anchor in Catalina Island coves, wrapped in a blanket to ward off the afternoon chill, and watched a bank of thick brown guck roll over the anchorage, blotting out the world around me while a true Californian sat in my cockpit and extolled the virtues of the state. To make matters worse, I agreed with him. But that was before I had seen Martha's Vineyard or Nantucket or Newport or Block Island or Annapolis or the Intracoastal Waterway or Man-O'-War or Hope Town or Stocking Island in the Bahamas or the Florida Keys or any one of a thousand delightful harbors, coves, anchorages, villages, rivers, islands, and assorted cruising grounds which California yachtsmen could not conceive of in their wildest dreams. It was before I discovered that the sky God gave us was blue, not dirty beige. It was prior to my discovery that eyes were not supposed to sting. And it was before I learned that water could be many shades, from pale green to brilliant blue and as clear as glass all the way to the bottom some thirty feet below.

I vividly recall the day we decided to break the California Commandment. We were huddled down below in our forty-one-foot yawl, flailing to keep warm as the late afternoon fog bank settled over us and the boats anchored around us disappeared from view. Dory said, "You know, I think I'd like to try living aboard full-time. But not here. Not in California. Like the song says, 'It's cold and it's damp.' I want to live on a comfortable boat where the sky is clear and the water warm and there are road signs advertising monkey farms and alligator wrestling and parrot jungles. I long for tropical breezes stirring the palm fronds while coconuts drop from tall trees and crack the skulls of senile codgers out for an evening stroll. I think I'd like to move back to Florida."

Back to Florida? I didn't know she'd ever been there, a fact that brought to light a couple of unaccounted years in her youth. It turned out Dory's father had been involved in the original Florida land boom back in the late twenties and she'd never forgotten the place. So, sitting there in Catalina's Cherry Cove, tears rolling down our cheeks, we vowed that if the smog ever lifted enough to find our way back to Newport Beach, we'd hie ourselves to Florida as fast as our little legs would allow. That was about eleven years ago and I can honestly say that we have never regretted it for a moment. But then I make it a point not to regret any decisions I've made. My philosophy has always been to go where I think I would like to be, stay there as long as I am satisfied, then move on.

Would we ever move back to California? If the day came when we could no longer live aboard a boat, we probably would return to the West Coast. On the whole, the weather is better for landlubbers, the people are generally more interesting and vital, the percentage of old codgers is lower than Florida's, and someday California may find a solution for smog.

At this stage of our lives we can't visualize ourselves living on-shore any more than we can consider moving back to California. Frankly, we've fallen in love with the East Coast and particularly with the watery part of Florida. If ever we do have moments of doubt, we simply have to look at that brilliant blue sky, those spectacular cloud formations, that green water, the thousands of protected coves and anchorages, the fish swimming under our boat impatiently waiting for us to drop a hook and pop them into a frying pan, the yachtsmen who spend their time cruising from one delightful spot to the next.

But we did spend twenty-five wonderful years in California and we never regretted a moment of it. We raised our kids in La Jolla and that's a tough act to top. We have lots of good friends in California who still ask us, "When are you coming back?"

Our answer is usually, "With luck, never. We hope to spend the next twenty-five years just as we are, living in a place that God must have meant for boating nuts, surrounded by people like ourselves, strong of back and fingers, healthy and happy, and still in love with life and each other. But if things should change, look for us. But don't count on it. We may have decided that Greece or Tahiti or Tierra del Fuego is our next paradise."

After all, it only requires untying the dock lines.

Rain in Heaven

⚓ *SEPTEMBER, 1980*

We live aboard our boat in the best spot on Fort Lauderdale's New River. We're on a bend where a cooling breeze blows even on the hottest days. Ashore lies a private patio shaded by a magnificent tree a hundred years old or more. Less than fifty yards away glimmers a fine swimming pool. Fifty yards in another direction stands the lovely old Riverside Hotel, with two excellent restaurants and a great little bar. We haven't heard the whine of a mosquito in the eighteen months we've been tied up here. An occasional foray with an insect bomb keeps the palmetto bug population to a minimum and our muscles in tone.

Ten boats are tied up along our dock, almost all of which are used as permanent residences. On rare occasions one of the boats will leave for a short cruise or to be hauled out. Mostly, we all just enjoy the closest thing to paradise we could hope for. There are no inconveniences. We like our neighbors and get along just fine. So, why do some of us spend a good part of our time griping about our lot?

Our closest neighbors are Sy and Vicki Carkhuff and their son, David. The Carkhuffs took five years out of their lives and girdled the world in a forty-foot yawl, then returned to what most people call the "real" world. They now live aboard a forty-two-foot trawler with four times the room and comfort.

Are we screwed up because we live aboard boats? Hell, no. We figure we are screwed up because we can't be content with what you and most other people would consider to be paradise. It *is* paradise! But the option to untie the lines and take off whenever the mood hits us makes us chafe under the restrictions we place on ourselves. The Carkhuffs have a twelve-year-old son who is in a private school, meeting kids under "normal" circumstances for the first time. They want him to have a proper education, to learn to get along with other kids in a typical environment. This is understandable.

Dory and I are high-school dropouts. I claim the distinction of being a totally uneducated, self-made pauper. Neither of our two daughters graduated from college and, from all appearances, nor will our granddaughter, Chelsea. We tell ourselves we stay because our daughter, Linda, lives two blocks away and needs us. But that's not true. She got along without us for ten years before she moved to Fort Lauderdale. No, it isn't that feeling of being needed that keeps us tied to the Riverside dock.

I think it's the knowledge that we have found the best of all possible worlds. To admit it would mean the impossible dream had been realized. And if we admit that, what can we look forward to?

Our boat is a fifty-two-foot power cruiser, built back in 1952 for a couple of brothers who wanted the boat set up to handle the owners in a master stateroom and infrequent guests. It's probably the best liveaboard arrangement you could find in fifty-two feet. We can't find anything to criticize, and we believe it is as good today as the day it was built. We couldn't duplicate it for ten times what we paid.

Vicki Carkhuff spends her days pecking away at her typewriter in air-conditioned comfort. I do the same on my boat. Almost every day at lunchtime Vicki, Dory, and I sit around the patio and have a bite to eat and some conversation. After Vicki and I compare our progress on whatever stories we are working on, the conversation drifts back to the number-one subject . . . our next cruise.

Vicki and Sy went around the world and want to do it again. Dory and I never got farther from land than midway between Palm Beach and West End in the Bahamas. That's about thirty miles in either direction. The Carkhuffs reminisce about Tahiti, New Zealand, and the like. We tell our adventures in the Abacos and Exumas. They recall thirty-five-day passages between landfalls. We are reminded of thirty-five minute trips via Zodiac from Man-O'-War to Hope Town for the Sunday brunch at the Harbor Lodge (with all the champagne you can drink). They enjoyed the long periods where just the three of them learned to rely on themselves and one another. We enjoyed a harbor where new boats are arriving and leaving every day, bringing us new conversations, books and magazines we haven't read, faces we haven't seen, and stories we haven't heard.

Most people go through life seeking security, avoiding changes of direction, burrowing deeper into their little fortresses, scheming and scurrying to make more money, and accumulating "things" that will prove they have achieved success. These are *normal* people. The Carkhuffs and the Bradleys are definitely not normal. We can be described as either abnormal or subnormal, depending on your viewpoint. Either way, neither the Carkhuffs nor the Bradleys really give a damn how we are perceived by normal society. We have become self-proclaimed outcasts and we look on our critics with pity. We understand their consternation when they walk down the dock and see what appear to be grown-up people living in the cramped quarters of small boats. They have a right to be amazed at our obvious disregard for the conventional mores of American society. We are a threat to everything they believe in and have worked for years to achieve.

To them the sturdy lines that hold us to the dock appear to be flimsy strings that might let go at the least provocation. To us those same lines are like bands of steel, handcuffs and leg-chains that keep us from wrenching loose from the noise and traffic and crime and triviality of everyday life ashore. We would probably be better off if our dock lines *were* made of steel and fastened to the dock in some permanent fashion. Then we could forget our dreams of breaking away and returning to what we perceive as being the "real" paradise that lies somewhere offshore. So, it becomes evident that our unhappiness with where we are is due to having the options of finding happiness in some other version of paradise.

But while each couple has its own excuse for being discontented, neither the Carkhuffs nor the Bradleys would chafe quite as much if we were not next-door neighbors. When you have two couples with the same fires banked deep inside, it doesn't require much to fan those coals into flames.

The solution then is obvious. One couple should move away and the slip become filled by folks who have enough sense to recognize paradise. The remaining couple could then slide into the normal Florida coma and begin that long, easy trip to senility and contentment. Who shall leave? Why, the Carkhuffs, of course. We were here at the dock first, our docklines are perfectly arranged, and they're planning to go farther than we are. So, they'll need a head start.

Besides, we've just signed up to get on the local cable TV system and . . . well, we have our reasons. But someday, by God, we're going to resume our search for paradise.

Survive the Savage River

⚓ *APRIL, 1979*

Don't tell me any of your sea stories. I don't give a damn about your single-handed transatlantic crossing, or how you rounded Cape Horn in a papyrus johnboat. Those are pieces of cake compared to what I go through almost every weekend on the New River in Fort Lauderdale.

Actually, there are three Fort Lauderdales. The best is the summer version, when slips at Bahia Mar and Pier 66 go begging, and the heat and humidity put the locals into a state of torpor. Then the New River is glassy smooth. The natives seldom venture out during the day, and the boats that do poke out go so slowly they hardly leave a ripple. About the only thing for me to complain about is that the ice melts too fast in my afternoon rum and Coke.

But then comes fall when the northern boats start arriving and Lauderdale turns into "Liquordale." The New River begins to toss a bit as the boating and boozing types see how much wake they can make for the "fat cats" in the big yachts tied up at the docks.

There is a generous exchange of obscenities as twenty-foot aluminum skiffs with twenty-year-old outboards plow along at the perfect speed to roll every boat along the route. Seldom have so many caused such misery for so few.

It isn't until the season starts that Fort Lauderdale metamorphoses a third time into "Fort Armpit." This is the time when a slip is fought over like Yemeni oil rights. Dockmasters are offered bribes. Millionaire yachtsmen are obsequious to dock boys. Traffic in the streets becomes impossible. Not just awful—impossible.

Everybody is teed-off. The weather is too cold to go to the beach. The water is too cold for swimming. Everybody has brought a head cold down from the north, and the natives are sneezing and coughing from too much contact with germ-ridden tourist dollars.

There is a constant churning as irate skippers mill around the

Fort Lauderdale during the season;
everybody is teed-off.

docks in their sixty-footers, claiming reservations that no one remembers or can find. Threats fill the air, and invitations to "step onshore and say that" are offered and accepted by normally serene members of the country's most decorous yacht clubs.

Adding to the confusion are the owners of the so-called macho boats. They're stamped out by cookie cutters: black, curly hair that owes a lot to Clairol and a blow dryer. Gold chains draped around flabby necks with giant sculptures resting on bronzed bellies. Bikini shorts, worn three sizes too small as optimistic proof of virility. Dark glasses a must. Lounging around are one or two bleached blondes with bombs bursting in air. Silver lamé Top-Siders mark the wearer as the skipper's first mate once removed.

As norther after norther blows through, the old salts along the river mutter vague threats about heading for the "islands." It is never made clear whether they mean the Bahamas, the Virgins, the atolls of the South Pacific, the Keys, or the now-vacated Manhattan.

Winter is also the time of the "maggots," as the local police affectionately refer to the younger immigrants. Decrepit vans holding a dozen or more unwashed escapees from northern reformatories find parking places in private lots and claim squatters' rights until forcibly removed by the *gendarmes*. During their brief stay, boat owners seem to lose small outboards, deck chairs, winsome daughters, and anything else that isn't nailed down.

Fortunately for all, the season is short-lived. The Snow Birds start readying their vessels for the trip north on the Waterway starting in mid-March. By April 15, the early birds will be bidding their dock neighbors farewell and heading slowly northward, having forgotten how miserable Long Island Sound can be in early May, when they are scheduled to arrive. It isn't really that they've forgotten; it's more that some people can only take Florida in small doses.

Others are encouraged to leave early by permanent residents who have plucked the Snow Birds clean and are now anxious to see only their tail feathers as they let the New River return to the way God and the Corps of Engineers meant it to be.

Then one day you wake up and there is a stillness that upsets you. You peek out the porthole and see only empty docks. The river is placid, and the current, true to form, is running a bit slower. The sound of traffic, the stench of gas fumes, the wails of ambulances and police cars are gone. You look at the calendar, and it says May, and then you know.

It's summer and the real Fort Lauderdale is back. And all is quiet on the river.

Thank God. It didn't come a minute too soon.

Any Excuse in a Storm

⚓ *SEPTEMBER, 1979*

This may come as a complete surprise to you, but the fact is a fuel shortage is a blessing in disguise for thousands of boat owners.

If you've ever spent much time wandering around marinas, you know how few boat owners actually use their boats compared to the number who spend their time working on them, partying on them, or using them as hideaways. I'd be willing to bet there are thousands of men out there who own boats but hate boating. The thought of untying the dock lines and heading out for open water is enough to chill them to the marrow.

Take my friend Lacey, who owns a beautiful old wooden yawl. He loves spending time on his yacht, talking with passersby about heading for some far-off paradise—but he really doesn't want to actually *do* it.

The truth is, Lacey likes it where he is, tied firmly to a dock while the world passes him by on its way to and from those places he says he'd like to see.

Lacey has the perfect boat for his needs. It's elderly and tends to develop strange maladies whenever departure day gets close. If it isn't his engine that needs overhauling, it's the bottom that needs paint, or a radio that is on the blink. On an old wooden boat the list is endless, and Lacey loves his list more than life itself. Nobody on his dock criticizes Lacey because we are all in the same situation. We've got our lines adjusted perfectly, our friends know how to reach us, shopping is close by and besides, where could we go that would be nicer than where we are?

Before the fuel shortage it was difficult and frequently embarrassing to answer questions concerning plans for future cruises. Lacey was able to fend off even the most persistent inquisitors by putting the blame on his vessel's deficiencies. But after two years at the dock, he was beginning to run low on excuses. Even his best friends were beginning to suspect that Lacey didn't want to go anywhere that required casting off his dock lines. His usual ploy was to have a chart of the Virgin Islands spread out in the cockpit with a big red circle drawn around St. Thomas. Somehow, Lacey managed to give the impression that he'd love to get "back to the island," but it was never made clear just which island he referred to.

I finally asked him one day if he were looking forward to getting back to the Virgin Islands. "Hell, no," he assured me. "I'd like to get my old slip back on Isle of Venice right here in Fort Lauderdale." That got me thinking. I was always saying that I'd like to get back to the Abacos in the Bahamas. But did I really? After all, it's at least a two-hundred-mile run, part of it across the Gulf Stream. Once I got there, what would I do? There is no phone. The mail is maddening. The market is poorly stocked, and the prices about double what they are right here. On the other hand, there is that beautiful clear water and those wonderful native Bahamians and all the folks we meet cruising.

Then the other day Dory asked me what we'd do if there weren't *any* fuel for boats. That thought hadn't occurred to me, although it is something every boat owner should be concerned about. Before answering her I thought for a while. What *would* we do if fuel dried up? The more I thought about it, the more I realized that we would do just what we are doing. We'd sit at the dock, look out on the river, swim in the pool, and enjoy our cocktails every evening on the bridge deck.

Not only that, I could subscribe to the Book-of-the-Month Club and I could get a library card and settle down to a life that would be half ashore and half afloat. Hey, that's what I've wanted all these years; to be able to straddle the distance between the two life-styles.

I voiced my thoughts at the nightly cocktail hour and discussion period that is held on the dock beside my boat. Everybody was there. Intrepid skippers every one, with hundreds of hours of sailing time beneath their keels. My question was simple: What would their reaction be to the news that there would be no fuel whatsoever for boats, forcing us to stay where we were until the knuckleheads in Washington got the mess straightened out?

Instead of being disturbed by such thoughts, as I suspected one or two might be, the reaction was one of great relief. Uncle Phil, whose lovely ketch is capable of sailing around the world, broke out in smiles and said, "I gave up planning a cruise two years ago. I like it where I am. But the fuel shortage makes it official."

So, here we sit. I've just checked the dock lines and found them secure and unchafed. We've put in a stock of charcoal and subscribed to the local newspaper. We're set for the summer at least. But does that mean we won't be cruising this year? Not on your life. We plan to visit our friends in the Chesapeake, and Long Island Sound, and Newport, and Boston. We'll visit them on their boats at their docks this summer, and when it's time to reciprocate, with luck, we'll be long gone and the fuel crisis will be just a fading memory.

Paradise Is Where You Find It

⚓ *JUNE, 1981*

There is nothing so devastating as to wake up one morning and learn that you have been suffering for most of your life from terminal stupidity.

I discovered my affliction not long ago when, after having searched diligently for ten years to find the end of the rainbow, I discovered the pot of gold was two days by boat from where I've been sitting. You see, Dory and I have been mildly discontented with our lot in life ever since we deserted southern California (where we were equally discontented) and headed east to Florida. We'd read Sloan Wilson's great book, *Away from It All,* and we'd absorbed countless articles in boating magazines extolling the benefits of a life afloat on what is called the Gold Coast. But after our arrival in Florida, we felt we'd been sold a share in a mine full of fool's gold.

For ten years we moved around from marina to marina, seeking a location we could honestly say fulfilled our dreams of what life should be afloat. We went north and we came south. We spent six pleasant months in the Bahamas Out Islands. We crossed the Gulf Stream again and again in our search for paradise. Occasionally, we thought perhaps we'd found it. But what appeared to be gold turned to gilt and then peeled off. Not that we were miserable, mind you, because we weren't. It's just that we weren't ecstatic. Do you know what I mean? And I have always figured, "What the hell, as long as I'm here on earth I might as well shoot for total bliss than settle for mediocrity."

During the countless hours of conversation we've had about where we wanted to go and what we'd hope to find when we got there, we have planned cruises to just about every place reachable by water except Tierra del Fuego. Then we'd draw up a list of reasons why we shouldn't go there and inevitably the list against was twice as long as the list in favor. So, we'd settle back and vegetate for another six months. But after staring at the muddy water of Fort Lauderdale's New River for over two years, we finally looked at one another and said, "Is this why we bought a boat and moved to Florida? Surely, in a state with a coastline that looks like it had been drawn by a snake with a nervous twitch, there has to be one harbor . . . one marina . . . that combines everything we came to Florida to find in the first place? Let's find it before we're too old to remember what we wanted."

We drove and explored and drove some more. We started at the northern tip of Florida (br-r-r-r, cold!) and made our way south to Fort Lauderdale. We finally settled on a rather small city some one hundred miles north of Fort Lauderdale. It wasn't really what we wanted but it was better than what we had. We announced to our friends that we were moving farther north and most of them admitted they were thinking of doing the same. The flight out of Miami and Fort Lauderdale to less troubled ocean communities is awesome and we were comforted to know that we weren't alone in our search. Having friends tell us they'd soon join us somewhat eased our concerns about leaving the dock we'd filled for almost three pleasant years.

Then a neighbor asked, "Have you tried the Keys? You'd love Key West." We admitted that we had only seen Key West once, and that was by car. Our neighbor kept urging us to at least have a look before making our big move. So, one early morning in March we started down the road that leads to America's southernmost city, pretty much convinced that we wouldn't like what we would see but dreading even more the thought of having to tolerate our neighbors' accusations of being inflexible and dumb for not trying, at least, to find something better than the city we had settled on. It was raining as we left and we agreed that it was better to see a new area on a bad day because, that way, you weren't bowled over by the bright sun or blue sky—we would see the place as it really was, warts and all. En route to Key West we stopped at every marina large enough to handle our fifty-two-foot Huckins, and the more we saw the less we liked. Then we hit pay dirt.

Friends had called a week before to say they were living aboard in a marina called Faro Blanco. Faro Blanco? Where was it, in Cuba? No, not Cuba, I was told; in the Keys and about halfway to Key West. When they offered to buy us a drink, treat us to dinner, and let us bunk on their boat, we figured it was well worth the effort to look them up. As it turned out, this visit was the best move we'd made in the past ten years. In the midst of a wide spot in the road called Marathon was the paradise we'd been trying to find.

"It reminds me of Ocean Reef, only not so stuffy," said Dory.

"Gee, it reminds *me* of Treasure Key in the Abacos, only better maintained," I answered.

"But the lighthouse makes me think of Hope Town," she went on.

"And the water reminds me of the banks between Man-O'-War and Hope Town," I said.

"Even the docks are kind of like the Conch Inn's in Marsh Harbor."

"But best of all," I said, "is that it's right here in the United States. No crossing the Gulf Stream in a norther!"

"No Customs to clear!"

"No lost mail or two-hour delays for phone calls."

"No paying double for beer and food!"

"Plenty of free water! Cable TV! The Sunday *New York Times!*"

"Clean laundromats! Great fishing right off the dock! Close enough to our daughter's house for visits but far enough to rule out babysitting!"

We were about to collapse in a fit of joy when the owner wandered by wearing scruffy Top-Siders and a pair of shorts.

"Pardon me, I'm a world-famous author and I'm considering moving to your resort. Can you tell me something about it?" I asked. (I was wearing a shirt a friend had given me. It says *Time* on the pocket and I sort of let the fellow think I was the editor.)

"Well, I don't recognize you or your name, but I'd be happy to put you up for the night in our lighthouse. Joe Namath moves out at five and you can move in around six, if you'd like. You'd be my guest, of course."

Of course. He probably saw through my little charade but felt sorry for Dory having to put up with such a braggart. We spent the night and woke up about seven to a brilliant blue sky and the putt-putt of a boat's engine. We tottered over to a window and looked out on a scene so breathtakingly beautiful we almost forgot about our hangovers. (While we didn't take up our friends' offer for bed and board, we had helped them destroy a fresh bottle of Canadian Club the night before.) There was a beautiful yacht slipping across an emerald-green sea, leaving in its wake a froth of white that was made even more brilliant by the cloudless blue sky. Directly below us the young dock attendant was catching snapper from the dock and I watched him pull in four in fifteen minutes.

I looked at Dory. She seemed mesmerized by the scene. Slowly, she turned to look at me. I could tell by her expression that our search was over. Paradise was right here, outside that window.

During breakfast we tried to be practical, exchanging such comments as, "We'd better think before we jump" and "There must be downside risks" and "Maybe we'd better come back in a month or so and look at it then." But we both knew we were playing a game. Each was waiting for the other to ask, "How soon do you want to move?"

An hour later we had picked out a slip with a view of the spectacular sunsets the Keys are famous for and by noon the next day we were aboard *Simba*, getting ready for the ninety-three-mile run down the Waterway to our new home.

As we enjoyed our cocktail that evening, Dory said, "Can you believe that Faro Blanco has been just sitting there while we've been scrambling around like idiots looking for it? How come you didn't find it ten years ago?"

"Look," I said, "isn't it enough I'm rich and famous? Do I have to be intelligent, too?"

"I'd settle for any one of those three qualities," answered my bride. "But I guess I'll have to settle for what I've got. And what more could a woman ask for than a husband who took her to paradise?"

Our Town

⚓ NOVEMBER, 1981

When we moved to Faro Blanco in the Florida Keys some months back, we got a number of letters and phone calls asking us how we thought we were going to adjust to life in a small town. I can assure you that adjusting to life here took about three days.

While both Dory and I were born and raised in Chicago, from the day we were married our primary goal was to live in a small community. We first tried a suburb of Chicago called Winnetka and then moved to Evanston, where we lived for several years. When I got out of the service in 1946, we decided to flee the Midwest and head for the West Coast. We settled eventually in a charming little seaside village called La Jolla, where we lived and raised our family for about sixteen years. Then we became bored with La Jolla and moved to Laguna Beach and, two years later, to Newport Beach. All of these started out as villages and suffered what chambers of commerce called "progress." I call it devastation.

When we decided to move to Florida and live aboard a boat full-time, we tried (and didn't like) Fort Lauderdale, Palm Beach (which we liked), Ocean Reef and, for six months, Man-O'-War Cay in the Bahamas. With the exception of Fort Lauderdale, most of these places could be described as villages or small cities. When we returned from the Abacos, we moved to a particular slip behind the lovely old Riverside Hotel on the New River. We seldom ventured beyond the hotel grounds except to shop or go to the library. We had good friends on the other boats along the dock and we were, to all intents and purposes, living in a very tiny village. But eventually the noise, dirt, traffic, crime, crowds, and twenty-four-hour wail of sirens wore us down. So, we searched for the next paradise and found it in Faro Blanco.

So, what's it like living in a small Florida Keys town? It ain't all that bad. We have everything necessary to sustain life as we think of it these days. A great restaurant on the marina grounds, and a dozen or more others ranging from seafood houses to Pizza Hut and International House of Pancakes. We have a huge supermarket, library, fine hospital, doctors, dentists, lawyers: every kind of service or retail outlet you could want. Not fifty bakeries, but at least one very fine bakery. And how much bread and pastry can you eat, anyway?

The people are friendly and, if a bit unsophisticated, so much the better. A little sincerity is worth a lot of sophistication any day. The Marathon Yacht Club is a small, unpretentious place but its members are friendly and very active boating enthusiasts. I haven't heard a siren wail since we've arrived. What crime there is is petty and the traffic is such that we can drive the three miles to the shopping center in less time than it used to take me to drive four blocks to the post office in Lauderdale. My blood pressure was 130 over 80 when I arrived in Marathon and it's now 120 over 80. That says something about life in the slow lane.

I'd forgotten how much fun it was to live in a marina where there was a mixture of year-round residents and transients. It makes for a nice blend of old and new friends and it means there is never a dull evening. If we wanted to, we could be busy every night down here. Parties, quiet dinners, a casual drink aboard someone's boat after dinner, or maybe my favorite . . . sitting on *Simba* and just staring out at all that natural beauty. And enjoying that much-touted Keys pastime, watching the sunsets.

What don't we have that I don't miss? We don't have fashionable stores, and I can assure you that is a blessing. Our bank balance has taken a turn for the better because of the absence of Saks, Burdines, and Jordan Marsh. As Dory says, "When you live in a bathing suit sixteen hours a day, who needs Saks?" I had to go to the doctor's not long ago and I put on a pair of underwear shorts for the first time in months. I felt as though I were wearing a tux! I haven't seen a man in a necktie since we got here and would view with suspicion any man I met so attired.

There's only one stop light in the whole village. If you're driving toward Key West and catch a green light you're apt to pass through town without knowing it. If you're a city slicker you're apt to look down your nose at Marathon and say, "Hick town! Rinky tinky!" And you'd be right. This is a rinky-tinky town. And that's why I love it. It isn't a phony anything, like so many medium-sized urban sprawls that call themselves cities.

I'm the kind of person who wants to be either in a *real* city like New York or Paris or Chicago or London, or else in a small community like Marathon. What I don't like is the in-between places that give you all of the drawbacks of a city with none of the advantages. But let me tell you something. The people who live in Marathon aren't rinky tinky. They're there because they feel like I do about the place. And if you look around you and ask, "What am I doing in this excuse for a city?" come on down and join us country folk for a while.

It's life in the slow lane. And it's wonderfully satisfying. Y'all have a nice day now, y'hear?

There's No Place Like Home
⚓ *SEPTEMBER, 1982*

Friends have often said to me, "There's no gray in your life, Bradley. It's either black or white, with nothing in between!"

They're right, I suppose. Dory and I do tend to go to extremes in just about everything we do. I guess we just dread finding ourselves missing something in life, some great experience or emotion, and so we shy away from the norm and look for the unusual or exciting. I've always felt that too many people settle for a life filled with fear and concern for the future or for the opinions of friends, family, or neighbors. That's never really bothered us a great deal. We've just done what we wanted to do and let others judge us as they wished.

When we decided to move to a quieter community, we moved to a *very* quiet place . . . Faro Blanco in the Florida Keys. It doesn't get much quieter than our little corner of the world. And we love it that way. Within a week of moving there we could feel the tensions fading away and the blood pressure dropping. Our nerves smoothed out and life began to make sense again. It's that kind of life-style that attracted us and pulls us back whenever we've been away for any length of time. We just heard from our friends the Bollings, and Bill's blood pressure is at an all-time low since he moved his boat to the slip directly behind ours. It's good to know that it works for others.

But Dory and I also love New York. I mean we really *love* New York. We spent ten weeks in that fascinating city this past spring and, while part of my time was spent undergoing and then recuperating from an operation, we were reminded once again that the center of the universe has to be in Manhattan. In fact, every time we visit New York, Dory will say, "If I had the money I'd like to live part of the year in New York, part in Faro Blanco, and the rest of the time I'd like to spend in the Hamptons or Newport or Europe." There's one thing about Dory, her dreams are never lacking in imagination.

Dory loves the Big Apple for the fabulous stores, and the beautifully dressed people, and the opportunity to walk and walk and walk. That's her only complaint about the Keys. There isn't much opportunity to take long walks. You tend to walk into either the ocean or the Gulf if you aren't careful. When in New York, Dory will walk miles and miles, window-shopping or strolling through Central Park or spending my hard-earned money in Bloomingdale's or Saks Fifth Avenue. Within a week of arriving in New York, she is walking faster, her eyes are brighter, she's bursting with energy, and she's better dressed.

My reasons for loving New York are somewhat different. I love to walk down Fifty-seventh Street and have Harry Belafonte give me a grin and a cheery "hello" or sit down to dinner in a tiny French restaurant and find Woody Allen at the next table. Or pass Dick Cavett on the street on a Sunday morning. I love looking at New York women because they are so spectacular. I love the sheer energy that fills the air in New York. Everybody works at top speed and with great efficiency.

I love the way people dress in New York. Dress ranges from the sublime to the ridiculous. One thing is certain, every New Yorker is determined to be an individual and he or she works at it twenty-four hours a day. The result is that small-town hayseeds like us find ourselves overwhelmed with the kaleidoscope of color and design that New Yorkers take for granted. There is no way a panel of experts could pick the 10 or 100 or 1,000 best-dressed people in New York because just about everyone is dressed best for him or her. And the women . . . the beautiful women. No other city in the world comes close to New York when it comes to gorgeous, spectacular, dazzlingly beautiful women. I love 'em.

When we come back from New York, it takes us weeks to adjust to the culture shock of seeing the best-dressed people in town decked out in sandals, faded K mart shorts, shapeless shirts, and straw hats that even a horse pulling a carriage through Central Park would turn down as beneath his dignity. Marathon, Florida, must be the only town left in America, other than Newport, Rhode Island, where the young men still wear their hair down to their shoulders. In fact, we have often wondered why a town so filled with pretty girls has so few attractive young men. If I were a thirty-year-old bachelor in search of a beautiful lady, I'd settle in Marathon. Fortunately, an overweight sixty-seven-year-old married man, whose wife keeps an eagle eye on him, doesn't have that problem.

After a week back in Faro Blanco, we have adjusted to the peace and once again discover we are looking forward to a spectacular sunset. And there are always late afternoons when we watch people cleaning their daily haul of grouper, dolphin, and snapper.

The day's highlight consists of a trip to the nearby shopping center with a stop at the library on the way. Early evenings are spent having a cocktail on a yacht in the marina. Then Dory explains her reasons for not wanting to cook (too hot, too tired, one missing ingredient for some particular dish) and we stroll up to the restaurant for dinner.

Quiet? You bet. The town's one movie theater is closed for the summer. The stoplight has been put on yellow for the slow season. How do we stand it, you may ask? The truth is, we don't. This summer we were in Paris, Nice, Amsterdam, London, New York, Newport, Rhode Island, Newport Beach, California, San Diego, and, in between, we cruised the canals of France and Holland. By mid-October, Faro Blanco will once again look like paradise to us. We'll be ready for some peace and quiet. Dory will be happy as a clam sanding and varnishing and I'll be content to sit back and admire all the local lovelies.

If "getting there is half the fun," getting back is the other half.

· FIVE ·

Rusting on My Laurels

Ups and Downs

⚓ *MAY, 1981*

I had a young fellow ask me a tough question the other day. "What should I major in, Mr. Bradley, so that I can spend my golden years sitting on my duff on a nice boat just like you're doing?"

I thought about that question for a while. It was obvious he was serious. I suppose my life-style does seem ideal to someone who isn't fully aware of the circumstances that brought me to this state. You see, what this young fellow doesn't know is that I am one of the all-time great fakers. I look prosperous. I talk prosperous. I act prosperous. But I'm actually poor as a churchmouse. How could I set this young fellow straight without destroying my image? I decided it couldn't be done. I'd just have to be honest with him.

"Let me ask you something, my young friend. How can you be so sure that I am enjoying financial security? What if I told you I existed on a day-to-day basis, wondering where next month's slip rent is coming from and how long I can stall off the credit-card people?"

"Oh, hell, I want to be laid back like you are, Mr. Bradley. I can tell you haven't a financial worry in the world." He said this with great enthusiasm and it was obvious he thought it was true.

"My laid-back demeanor," I told him, "is not due to relaxation as much as it is to being in a state of perpetual shock caused by hypertension, which is the result of my bride asking me, on a daily basis, if I have any idea of where our next meal is coming from."

"That's hard to believe, Mr. Bradley."

"Talk to my wife. There's hardly a day goes by when she doesn't say, 'I can't believe we're overdrawn again. I just deposited two thousand dollars the day before yesterday?' "

He looked at me with disbelief.

"How can you be poor? You live on this nice yacht. You wear nice clothes. You have a nice car. I've seen you dining in fine restaurants. How can you claim to be a pauper with all that?"

I gave him a superior smile and answered, "You've hit it right on the head, young man. It's all *that* that has brought me to this lowly state. I lived for many years thinking I was young. I was sure that life would go on forever. I didn't think about losing my youth or my energy. The world was made for me and me alone. When Dory said, 'I like that dress,' I bought it for her. If she said, 'This boat is too small,' I bought her a bigger one. When she chided me for spending every penny, I said, 'Nonsense! I haven't yet hit my stride. My big earning years are still ahead.' "

Do I make it sound as if it were Dory's fault? I shouldn't. She has been after me for the past forty-two years to think about the future. But the future always remains the future until it suddenly becomes the present. The trick, as Satchel Paige used to say, is to never look back because something may be gaining on you. I mean, the last I remember I was about thirty-five and playing tennis at the La Jolla Beach and Tennis Club. The next thing I discover I'm eligible for Social Security. They've got to be kidding! Social Security? Me? Someone's made a mistake. Why, I've *seen* people who are on Social Security. They're old and wrinkled. Me, I'm still as vital and vigorous as I ever was. Well, maybe not quite. But certainly not old. Never old.

And Dory! Hey, dress her up and I wouldn't trade her for Bo Derek. She's not only gorgeous, she's smart. And best of all, she loves me as much as I love her. Don't try to tell me she's old. It won't wash. But how do I explain to this callow youth that I am a faker. Maybe one of the all-conference fakers. How do I explain to him that someday he may be sitting on a comfortable yacht in this same spot on the New

River, wondering what trick of magic to perform to get the bill collectors off his back. Wondering what soft-shoe routine he can pull off to take the worried look from his beloved wife's face?

"You see, young fellow, somewhere along the line you have to make a decision. You have to elect to get on the merry-go-round and put in your time, saving your money, investing it wisely and planning for that magic day when some young fellow says, 'Sorry, mac, you're fired. We're putting young Farthingill in your spot. Now you can take it easy for the rest of your life.' Or you can turn your back on that merry-go-round and ride the roller coaster, careening round the curves, and screaming down the dips while your stomach tries to come out through your mouth only to be followed by a climb to the heights where you think your hair is going to leave your head. It's simply a matter of making a decision that will alter your life forever."

He hesitated a moment, then said, "I guess I know which ride you decided to take, Mr Bradley. Tell me, would you do it all over again?"

"You bet your bippie I would, sonny. Do you know why? Because the ride is still a long way from over. I'm doing pretty much the same thing I was doing back when I was thirty-five. I'm surviving every day and looking forward to the next. I'm still on that roller coaster and when you see me sitting in my helmsman's chair, gripping the arms, and with my head resting on the back, you think I'm relaxed and laid back. But you're wrong, my boy, you're dead wrong. I'm hanging on as we ride a sharp curve. It's an exciting ride. Know why? Because I chose a roller coaster that never repeats itself. Every turn is different. Every twist and turn is new and exhilarating."

"It sounds like a great life for you, but how does Mrs. Bradley feel about this roller coaster way of life?"

"Let's ask her. Dory! Can you come up here for a minute? This young man would like to ask you a question."

Dory came up onto the bridge, looking great as always. The young man turned to her and said, "Mrs. Bradley, your husband has been telling me about your life on the roller coaster. Do you have any regrets? Anything you wish you'd done differently?"

Dory thought for a moment, a frown on her face. Then she nodded and said, "Yes, I think there is something I'd have done differently if I'd known what was ahead."

He gave me a triumphant look, thinking he had me. Then he asked, "What was it you'd like to do over?"

"Well," Dory answered, "I gave away a beautiful black Ceil

Chapman gown that Dick bought me back in about 1955. It would be perfect for today's fashions. I wish I'd kept it. But other than that, I can't think of a thing."

I asked him if he had any other questions.

Smiling, he turned to me and said, "Just one. Where do I buy a ticket for the roller coaster?"

Captain Video

⚓ APRIL, 1980

Last fall I got a phone call from an old friend suggesting that I appear before a group of electronics dealers to discuss the marketing of stereos and video recorders to the "over-fifty market."

"Since when is Madison Avenue interested in the over-fifty market?" I asked.

"Since they found out that the 'under-fifty market' was getting its spending money from the over-fifty market," my friend explained.

"Geez, I could have told them that ten years ago. Why didn't they come to me back then? I could have saved them millions of dollars," I told him.

"They wouldn't have listened ten years ago because their research told them the future was the youth market. But now research has done an about-face and everybody is trying to jump on the new bandwagon," I was told. "Besides, this is your chance to tell them how dumb you think they are."

"Where is this convention?" I'm sort of fussy about where I go these days.

"It's in Las Vegas."

"God, I detest Las Vegas. It's my idea of the armpit of America. But assuming I overcome my distaste long enough to go there, what am I supposed to do once I arrive?"

"Just appear on a panel with Gloria Steinem, who's going to talk about the female market. You'll be talking about the fifty and over market and somebody else will talk about the under-fifty market. It'll be a snap for you and you can have a nice trip and pick up some fast bucks. How can you miss?" My friend was very persuasive.

Well, to make a long story a bit shorter, I agreed to make an appearance, figuring that while I didn't know much about the over-fifty market, I sure as hell knew as much about my subject as Gloria Steinem knew about women. I've always looked at *Ms* magazine as the last resort for women who wished they'd been born men and I consider their readership to be about as average as that of *Horn Rim Monthly*. It would be fun tangling with the likes of her.

But then I discovered that I was to do a thirty-minute stand-up talk in which I discussed what made the over-fifty buyers different from those under fifty. I gave it a lot of thought and decided that the only difference was that one group was older than the other and probably smarter and more careful how it spent its money. But I couldn't stretch that out to thirty minutes. The next thing I knew they were telling me they wouldn't pick up Dory's air fare and she was telling me she wouldn't fly to Las Vegas under any circumstances. Well, I don't go anywhere without my Dory by my side, so that put a crimp in the operation.

Then they had that awful fire at the MGM Grand Hotel and I got to thinking what a shame it would be to fly to Las Vegas to make a talk I didn't want to make and then get killed in a fire. It was beginning to look as though this whole thing were not my cup of tea. Finally, I got a call from the agency telling me I would get the top-of-the-line video recorder for my appearance. That was about $1,300 for a half-hour talk. I was tempted. But Dory set me straight.

"How big is this video recorder?" Dory asked.

"Oh, about yea big," I told her, holding out my hands to give her some idea of its size.

"Where will we put it?" she asked.

I looked around the cabin of our boat and finally admitted we didn't have room for a video recorder. But she had more to say.

"Assuming we found space for it, what would you record?"

"Well," I answered, "I'd record shows that were on when we're out or that came on while we were watching a show on another channel."

"When was the last time there was something on TV you wanted to record?" When Dory sets her mind to something, she's a bear cat.

"I can't think of anything right off, but I'm sure I could find something to record. After all, every now and then there's something pretty good on TV." I don't give in easily.

"Let's leave it this way," she told me. "When you can think of three shows in the last year you would like to have recorded, I'll agree to let you fly off to that awful town and make a fool of yourself in front of a bunch of strangers and bring back a piece of electronic gear we haven't room for and will never use. You have until Christmas."

By the end of the week I knew I had lost. I couldn't come up with a single show I had liked enough to record nor could I think of a single show I had missed that I would want to see. I thought about the crummy looking people and the ugliness of Las Vegas and the weird life-style. I compared it with my boat and the pleasant life I live on the New River. I pictured myself standing up in front of a bunch of TV dealers who were hungover from last night's debauchery and whose minds were on getting to the slot machines as soon as possible. I heard my voice saying, "Gentlemen, the only difference between the over-fifty market and the under-fifty market is that we older folks are too damned smart to buy what you have to sell until you prove that it works like you say it does and you guarantee to service it if it doesn't work and it will take a lot more than your normal pitch to talk us into buying something we don't need and can't afford. My advice to you is to concentrate on those under-fifty buyers because they haven't learned enough yet to say no. And as far as what Ms. Steinem has told you, I doubt if she'd recognize a normal, everyday woman if she met one. So, why don't you run back to the slots and enjoy your stay in Las Vegas because I'm hauling my withered butt out of this place as fast as I can get to the airport."

The next thing I knew, Dory was giving me a nudge.

"You're moving your lips again. Whom are you talking to now?"

"Oh, I was thinking about what would happen if I made that talk in Las Vegas. I have a feeling it wouldn't work out."

She gave me a sharp look and said, "Don't waste your time think-ing about it. You're not going and that's final. I'm not letting you get out there with all those naked women. God knows what might happen to you!"

Gee, I hadn't thought about that aspect. The next thing I knew I was dreaming about being cornered in a hotel room by a half-crazed young woman, totally naked and fighting for my purity. I could feel my strength waning even as hers seemed to increase. Then just as I was about to give in . . .

"Your lips are moving again, Now whom are you talking to?"

I gave her my Mona Lisa smile and said, "Nobody, my sweet. I'm just planning my next column."

What the hell? If Jimmy Carter fantasizes, why not me? And at my age, it's all in my mind, anyhow.

Or is it?

Puzzling It Out

⚓ *NOVEMBER, 1982*

The only concern I've ever had about my life was the fear that I would somehow miss having the maximum number of experiences Fate had in store for me. When I reached fifty, I looked at my friends and decided too many of them were playing it safe, protecting what they had, and turning down opportunities to take on new challenges. I was talking to a buddy one day about the subject and came up with what I call my "Rickety Card Table" philosophy. Then I described what really happened as we made our way through life.

"When we're born," I said, "that old-fashioned cardboard table with rickety folding legs is set up in front of us, then God dumps a huge jigsaw puzzle on the table and says, 'OK, sort it out. And when it's finished you'll understand why you're here.' "

I went on to explain how all of us spend much of our time working on the puzzle in an effort to make some sense or reason out of what has happened along the way.

Eventually, the day arrives when a person puts the last piece in place and stands back to say, "Ah ha! Now I understand."

By the time this event occurs, it is quite likely that the person has reached middle age and is content to maintain a status quo posture. Having figured out over a period of fifty or more years what life was all about, they are not about to start all over.

The result of this is that most people spend the rest of their lives protecting the rickety card table. When someone gets near it they panic and fight to keep the intruder from bumping it, spilling the puzzle onto the ground, perhaps taking with it the clear picture of life's meaning. Perhaps you've been doing the same thing, assuming you have your puzzle worked out. If you haven't, what I'm about to suggest might not have much meaning to you.

When I reached fifty, my puzzle was beginning to form a hazy outline. I found my friends saying to me, "Bradley, you've got it made. Your life is all figured out. It must be great to just sit back and let life blow by. I envy you."

It so happened that each time I heard those words, I was in a state of boredom. I didn't look forward to protecting my card table; I wanted a brand new puzzle. I then did something that shocked my friends. I stepped back from my table and kicked the bottom, scattering the pieces all over hell and gone. I then looked up and said, "OK God, shoot me down another puzzle."

From then on, about once every five years I found myself kicking the table and calling for a new puzzle. It wasn't always easy to do. Life was comfortable and relatively secure. However, my friends would assure me that I had it made and when this happened I would question once again if having it made was what life was all about.

So Dory and I would talk it over and decide the time had come to look for new challenges, experiences, and more friends. This invariably required moving to a new location and starting fresh. It meant developing new clients and settling into a new community. It was fun and exciting and I think it kept us young beyond our years. With each move we built friendships that have lasted throughout the years, and I can say with all honesty that some of our very dearest friends are those we've met during the past two years, particularly since we have moved to Faro Blanco in the Florida Keys. People are so kind and thoughtful in this little patch of paradise that we are frequently overcome with gratitude. We are firmly convinced we'll be here for a long, long time. There just isn't any good reason to leave. Not even when a friend comes by and says, "Bradley, you've got it made."

The water is a brilliant green and the sky an equally brilliant blue. The fishing is fantastic right off the docks. And offshore a mile or so is a reef where grouper abound. Does it sound as if I'll be protecting my card table from now on? Not really. The fickle foot of Fate may come along and kick it out from under me, despite my best efforts to guard it. That's the one element I didn't take into consideration way back when I started to develop this corny philosophy. Having been in the hospital three times in the past year, I just can't forecast what the future has in store. But I'm so glad Dory and I have spent the past eighteen years kicking the bottom of that old card table. We've had a fantastic life with never a dull moment. I wonder how many of you can honestly say the same. I hope most can say yes. If you can't, try kicking the table.

Rusting on My Laurels

⚓ *OCTOBER, 1978*

After reading enough of my columns, you probably came away with the idea that this guy Bradley is a shrewd huckster who ratholed his substantial earnings over a period of thirty years, and then opted for early retirement and a hedonistic life-style on a remote tropical island. If you got that impression, let me set the record straight.

Just for starters, let's take a look at early retirement. Retirement is a condition which comes about when a man reaches sixty-five and is either fired or rich enough to do what he damned well pleases. Unfortunately, I don't come under either of these classifications. When I closed the doors of my advertising agency in 1974, it was because I simply got bored with what I was doing and quit.

Perhaps you're feeling the same way. If so, let me give you a word of warning. It ain't easy. Particularly if, like me, you come from a long line of free-spending Irishmen who never left their heirs anything but an overdrawn bank account. Not wanting to besmirch a perfect record, I followed in their footsteps and spent every dime I could earn.

The result was that on the day of my "retirement" I had just enough money to last through the month. Recalling my grandfather's advice ("A moving target is hard to hit"), I figured my best bet was to get out of town. After all, why worry my creditors with the news I was no longer solvent? But where to go was a problem. It isn't easy to be inconspicuous when you're living aboard a De Fever 50 trawler. Then I remembered that the America's Cup would be held in Newport that summer. What a perfect place to go unnoticed in a $150,000 yacht! The next day, we were on our way.

I hadn't gotten around to telling all my clients that I was no longer in business, and because they didn't expect much from me at best, they just kept sending checks which a friend picked up and forwarded. With nothing to do and money coming in, 1974 was a great year for the Bradleys. By the end of the summer, my wife convinced me that the bubble was about to burst, however, so I quickly sold the trawler, bought a more modest sailboat, and fled the frozen North. I discovered many years ago that poverty is an inconvenience in a gentle climate, but a tragedy when the temperatures drop below freezing.

I said that I was lacking in funds. But I did have a wife who was fascinated to see how things would turn out. To show her support, she burned all her credit cards except those from Saks and Bloomingdale's. I was allowed to keep a Sears card, but admonished not to use it. Her explanation was, "You've always told me not to let a shortage of money interfere with our style of living." What could I say? She also coined a phrase she has used over and over during these past eight years: "You don't need it." Never "I don't need it." She defends her position with, "You wanted to be a boat bum, so you can dress like one."

Eventually, we switched from a sailboat to a fifty-two-foot power cruiser, 1952 vintage, and found our way to the Abacos. Here we discovered that we could almost make ends meet, provided I kept busy writing and working as a consultant for boat builders in worse shape financially than I was.

As far as I'm concerned, the Abacos are a delightful place to spend a winter of apprehension. I think "apprehension" is a better word than "worry." I trained myself not to *worry* about money shortages. I let my wife do that and she's an expert at it. Hardly an hour goes by that she doesn't say to me, "I don't hear the typewriter clacking. Remember, no clacky, no checky."

There's one more point I'd like to clear up. The editor of *Motor Boating and Sailing* wanted to give me a steady job recently. But what he really had to offer was an ancient desk and a more ancient typewriter, with the suggestion that I give him a hand in exchange for an occasional lunch. I tried it for one day and discovered that lunch came from a cart filled with day-old rolls and battery-acid coffee. That was enough for me. As I told him, "I may not be Norman Mailer, but I do have my standards."

Well, it's 4:30 P.M. and time for a bit of rum and tonic.

"Honey, can I have my cocktail now?"

"You don't need it!"

What did I tell you?

Life at the Top

⚓ *NOVEMBER, 1979*

If there's one thing that has bugged the hell out of me for a long time it is the arrogance of wealthy yachtsmen.

For more years than I care to remember, I've been subjected to the humiliation of anchoring my boat in some harbor, proud as a peacock of the fact that it was a shade larger than anything else in the anchorage, only to have some huge gold-plater roughly twice our length come sliding in with uniformed crew poised on the foredeck, a professional captain at the wheel, and the owner's party sipping champagne in the cockpit, displaying a superior air that drove me up the wall.

"What gives them the right to steal my thunder?" I have often asked myself. "What have I done (or not done) to deserve my fate?" And I have then gone on to assure all within listening distance that I wouldn't want a boat that size, even if I could afford it. And I meant it from the bottom of my heart.

But something happened not long ago to cause me to rethink my position. What happened was that I had a chance to play wealthy yachtsman and, God forgive me, I liked it. I liked it!

It all came about as a result of my having played yacht broker for a while last winter and having sold a magnificent eighty-two-foot Rhodes ketch to a man with more millions than I have birthdays. During the negotiations, the owner and I became friends, primarily because we are both curmudgeons, are about the same age, have unruly beards and shaggy haircuts, and share an intense dislike of the yacht brokers with whom we were forced to deal with negotiating the sale.

How often does a guy get a chance
to fulfill a fantasy?

The friendship was furthered by the fact that the owner was a West Coast resident and Dory and I were the only people he knew on the East Coast. In a moment of blurred thinking, brought on by the consumption of a half bottle of fine champagne (I had consumed the other half), my friend had extended, and I had quickly accepted, an invitation to cruise aboard his yacht in New England during the summer.

We had only been aboard the yacht a few moments when I realized that it wouldn't take much to convert me from the meek, unassuming soul that I am into an arrogant, overbearing character worthy of flying the burgee of the you-know-what yacht club, whose members are required by charter to breathe only rarefied air which is several centimeters higher than normal breathable air and thus requires a certain tilt of the proboscis at all times. I'm not certain what it was that tipped me over the brink, but the truth is that within the hour I was strutting around the deck wearing my blue blazer, red pants, brown deck shoes and no socks, and an ascot around my neck.

I suppose I was influenced by the presence of several crew members who seemed poised at all times to fill my glass with champagne or serve me a delectable lunch. The thought that setting sail required only a murmured suggestion to launch the crew into action while I languished behind the wheel had a lot to do with my change of attitude. By the second day I was playing the role to the hilt, even to the point of pretending to be the owner (something which finally caused the owner to suggest that we take turns accepting the compliments of passing skippers). After a week Dory suggested that we think about leaving and heading back toward Florida, but I turned down the thought on the basis that we owed it to the owner to brighten up his life with our sparkling personalities.

By the end of the second week I detected a slight change in our host's attitude. Where he had been asking us how long we could stay, he now inquired in an off-hand way how soon we might be leaving. Not wanting to hurt his feelings and leave him alone on this giant vessel, surrounded only by his crew and half the lonesome ladies of New England, I said we could stay one more week. With that he took off in his plane and promised to return in time to say good-bye.

Even though I got the message, I figured, "What the hell! How often does a guy get a chance to fulfill a fantasy?" While he was away, I invited everyone I knew in Newport to join us for cocktails, took the boat out sailing, and generally lived the good life to its fullest. To this day there are people in Newport who think I must have inherited a fortune. I even had the crew fooled for a while. But this last achievement was also my undoing. When the owner returned a day early, he discovered the Owner Aboard flag was flying and as he walked down the dock the crew raised the Guest Aboard flag. While I can understand how he could have been slightly miffed, I see no excuse for his invitation for me to disembark immediately. Nor do I understand his fit of pique when he discovered we had consumed a full case of Bollinger's Brut champagne and several bottles of Chivas Regal. After all, we had brought two six-packs of beer aboard!

So, now we're back aboard *Simba* in Fort Lauderdale. For some strange reason the old girl seems to have shrunk somewhat during our absence. I suppose I'll get used to normal living eventually, but it won't be easy. I find myself reaching for the button that summoned the steward or opening the refrigerator expecting to find a round of Brie awaiting. But it didn't take Dory long to return to real life, she being the practical member of the family. Just a moment ago I asked if she'd put the Bollinger on ice. Her answer was as you might expect.

"Would you settle for a lukewarm Schlitz?"

Forever Young

⚓ *AUGUST, 1980*

When I was but a young lad, a kindly uncle asked me what I wanted to be when I grew up. It is told that my answer was prompt and to the point.

"I want to be very, very old."

On reaching sixty-five (that's years, not miles per hour), Dory, my bride of forty-one years, asked me a similar question.

"How old do you want to be when you grow up?"

I gave her the same answer: "Very, very old!"

You see, I abhor maturity. I've never liked "grown-ups" and have never wanted to spend much time with them. They bore the living hell out of me. Being grown-up means having stopped growing and anyone who deliberately wants to stop growing is eligible for inclusion on my list of people I don't want to spend time with.

Age has nothing to do with it. Some of the most boring grown-ups I know are in their early thirties. Some of the youngest, more vital people I know are likely never to reach a fully grown-up condition. I hope not, because I'd hate to add their names to that list. My struggle to keep from growing up hasn't been easy. Not growing up is like being un-American. Teachers, preachers, and presidents all hammer at you to "grow up, for God's sake!" Why? What's so great about growing up?

Growing up, grown-ups will tell you, means recognizing your responsibility to your family and community and state and country. Hey, I recognize those responsibilities. I've faced up to most of them, having served a short time in the military service, raised two daughters, paid a small fortune in income taxes, and exercised my rights as a citizen by voting against Tricky Dick consistently since first I laid eyes on his pinched face. Isn't that enough? Or must I assume responsibility for Jimmy Carter's boo-boos? And Ford's, before him? No, you can't con me into growing up with that spiel.

All these past forty-one years, as Dory and I blithely wended our way from one delightful community of well-off people to the next, being part of the group, and enjoying their kindness and generosity, more grown-up friends asked, "What will you do when you've grown up and discover you haven't put anything away for a rainy day?" My answer has always been the same. "I'll buy an umbrella for two and Dory and I will spend our time singing in the rain." Meantime, I intend to live every day to the fullest.

So, here we are. I'm sixty-five and I still haven't fully grown up. Along the way I've earned a lot of money and spent every dime. Do I regret it? Are you kidding? I wouldn't change a thing. Well, there was one year when I bought twelve—that's right, twelve—different cars. If I had it to do over again, I wouldn't have bought that Hudson Terraplane. It was really a dog. Outside of that I can't think of a thing I'd do differently.

Now my friends are saying, "You're a senior citizen and you still haven't decided on a career, you still haven't built a nest egg, and you still haven't grown up. What's going to happen to you and Dory? Doesn't it worry you?"

Frankly, no. We've got a twenty-eight-year-old boat that will probably last for another twenty-eight years. By then Dory and I will be in our late eighties and I'll be having a helluva time finding the typewriter keys. In fact, I'll have trouble finding the typewriter. So, we plan to take our boat to the Bahamas and drop anchor in the clear blue waters of the Abacos. Twice a year we'll come back to Florida to remind ourselves why we went over there in the first place.

We'll spend our days reading, chatting with the thousands of interesting cruising people who pass through the Bahamas on their way to far-off places, swimming off the stern, doing a bit of fishing to hold down food costs, doing a bit of drinking to keep our view of world events from becoming too gloomy, enjoying occasional dinners at the Conch Inn in Marsh Harbor, running up to Green Turtle to visit friends and down to Little Harbor for a change of scenery. When we become curious as to what's happening stateside we'll turn on our radios and form images in our minds far more colorful than the TV screen is capable of producing.

With any luck we'll maintain our carefree and irresponsible view of the world and our reason for being part of it. With the help of a few friends we'll make good use of every moment of our remaining years on this mixed-up planet. And, with a little luck, when our time comes to move on to another world we'll be overdrawn at the bank and owe the IRS several hundred thousand dollars, although that latter wish is beyond my imagination at the moment.

If and when I do finally grow up, I would like to look over a glass of champagne at my beautiful wife and say, "Happy ninety-fifth birthday, Darling! May next year be the best year of your life."

How I Spent My Summer Vacation

⚓ *DECEMBER, 1981*

"Wait a minute! Wait just a damn minute! Somebody's made a mistake. You've come for the wrong guy. This is Lucky Dick Bradley, the fellow who's never even been in a hospital in his entire sixty-five years, except as a visitor."

It was 7:45 A.M., Thursday, July 30, 1981, and I was surrounded by nurses, aides, and a few sightseers. Right in the middle of my protest someone stuck a needle into my butt and I was lifted out of my bed and onto a rolling contraption just like they used on *Dr. Kildare.* As I was rolled out of my room into the hall, my rapidly fuzzing mind told me that it wasn't a mistake. This was the moment of truth. The surgeon really was going to operate. My last recollection was feeling Dory's lips on my cheek and hearing her whispered assurances that everything was going to be all right. Then I floated off into dreamland.

What happened next is a total mystery. I slept peacefully while a gaggle of doctors and nurses and technicians bustled around my supine form, doing whatever doctors and nurses and technicians do best in similar circumstances. The next day, as I struggled back to consciousness, I opened my eyes to see Dory's pretty face and hear her voice telling me the operation had been a success. Slowly the fuzziness cleared and I discovered I was in the Intensive Care Unit, although it looked more like a set from an old British comedy, *The Man in the White Suit.* Remember how the British loved to use Rube Goldberg machines that gave forth strange burping, gurgling, and flatulent sounds? This place had it all.

As I rolled my eyes around I discovered that most of the strange noises were coming from machines that were attached to me by tubes. I looked like the star of a new TV series entitled *The $5,000 Hydraulic Man.* There were tubes to feed me and tubes to drain me. There were bottles above me and tanks below me and pumps in between that required frequent attention . . . usually between the hours of 10:00 P.M. and 5:00 A.M. I couldn't turn or twist or move a muscle without being reminded that I was a captive of modern medical science. So, I resigned myself to a few weeks of total rest and relaxation. But no sooner had I closed my eyes for a little nap than a nurse named Mary nudged me and said, "C'mon, honey, we're going to get you up for a little while. You've been asleep long enough."

Get me up? Was she kidding? I had trouble lifting my eyelids much less moving a muscle. "You mean I've been asleep for a whole week?" I asked. Mary assured me it was the day after the operation and time to get a move on. Somehow, Mary and a couple of helpers got me into a wheelchair, where I sat holding my stomach (which I was convinced would tumble down to the floor if I let go for even a second) and stared at a blank wall. When Dory came in a few minutes later she asked me what I was staring at so intently. "Television," I answered. At this she gave a sigh of relief and said, "Well, at least you've still got a sense of humor."

That afternoon they moved me into a private room that my good friends Bill and Patsy Bolling had given me as a birthday present.

("There's no point in inflicting Dick's miserable disposition on some innocent roommate," was Bolling's way of putting it.) The next time I opened my eyes I almost panicked. There were so many baskets of flowers and potted plants in the room I thought I'd died and had been transferred to a funeral parlor. But then Dory came in, kissed me and said, "Happy birthday, Darling," and I knew I was all right. Well, maybe not totally all right but at least alive and kicking. Any lingering doubts were dissipated the first time I coughed. What a sensation! From that moment on, my sole objective was to avoid coughing. Even though my doctor had assured me the stitches could not be ripped open and that the healing process would take hold in a couple of days, my naturally suspicious nature led me to remain as motionless as possible.

Of course, lying motionless is exactly what you aren't supposed to do. "Move around!" the nurses said. "Take walks and sit up in a chair!" Then would follow a period of gamesmanship as I did everything in my power to stay in bed and they prodded and nagged me to move around, sit up, take a walk. For a few days I stalled the morning shift by assuring them I'd walk in the afternoon. Then I'd tell the afternoon shift I'd walked three miles that morning and was just too tired to do more. It worked until the nurses recognized a gold brick when they saw one, and from that moment on I was on the way to recovery, modern-style.

Much to the horror of my city friends, I'd chosen to have my repair work done at Fisherman's Hospital in Marathon, Florida. Why? Because it was a two-minute drive from Faro Blanco, where we live aboard our boat. As it turned out, it was a wise decision. Just about everybody in Marathon is into boating. My radiologist and surgeon both read my column. Half the nurses were sailors. The place was not the typical factory where patients are simply numbers on a board. Not only that, the nurses were gorgeous and warm-hearted and they really cared about their patients. My personal guardian angel was named Jackie and she was a beautiful blond with a smile that could brighten the darkest of days. When Jackie was on duty I knew I'd be okay, and if you don't think that isn't important, you've never been in a hospital as a patient.

Then there was Joan, who shaved me "from knees to nipples" and carried on a lively conversation about sailing the entire time. I could go on and on, because the nurses (both female and male) were truly angels. During my two-week stay I came to appreciate what they do and, believe me, they richly deserve whatever they are paid . . . and more. Not that I was always glad to see them walking into my room, however. Particularly about 2:00 A.M., when they came in to check my vital signs, or when they came with needles seeking blood samples. Or the time when a new nurse's aide came in and woke me up at midnight to ask if I needed something to make me sleep. I wanted to say, "Yes, a lock on my door." But I didn't because she didn't appear to have a sense of humor . . . and she was carrying a needle at the time.

Most of the time I was there I was on a fluid diet, which had to be the most tasteless, unappetizing collection of food ever assembled. I mean, how can you screw up a bowl of Jell-O? I got so desperate I'd have welcomed an airline dinner. When I heard one day that the head cook had not shown up for work I assumed some ex-patient had assassinated him in the hospital parking lot. No jury would have convicted the murderer, not if the defense attorney had the jury run a taste test. Life was not made easier when I turned on my TV set, because fully 75 percent of the commercials were for food. How I longed for a bucket of Kentucky Fried Chicken or a Pizza Hut Super Pizza with the works! As might be expected, Dory came to my rescue and smuggled in malted milks and other goodies.

When I asked my doctor when I could return to *Simba,* he said, "As soon as you've passed wind." It's kind of embarrassing to have everyone in the hospital sticking their heads in the door asking, "Any luck yet?" When the big moment arrived there were cheers in the hall, my surgeon smiled for the first time, and a huge party was thrown in my honor at Faro Blanco's marina. Two days later I was released and assured that with a bit of luck and the miracles of modern medicine I should be typing this column twenty years hence.

While I don't recommend an operation as the perfect way to break up the summer doldrums, I will admit that it had its good sides. I was moved . . . really moved . . . by the letters and cards and flowers and phone calls that flooded in. In fact, at one point I broke down and cried like a baby (or a senile curmudgeon) because of the expressions of love and concern from friends and strangers alike. I discovered how sweet life is and found myself asking only that I be allowed to continue to live it exactly as I have been, aboard my old boat, surrounded by fine neighbors, and with my Dory at my side. And barring getting run down by a truck, the thought that I'll be around to enjoy this life for some years to come makes me feel like letting a tear slip down my bearded cheek.

I never said I was a macho type. At best, I see myself as a pussy-cat with the roar of a lion. And dammit, I've earned the right to sniffle when I want to.

"Dory, where'd you hide the Kleenex?"

Life Really Begins at Sixty-five

⚓ *JUNE, 1982*

Somewhere along the line we've blown it.

Just about the time a fellow has figured out what life is all about and how to do his job right, he's turned out to pasture and doomed to spend the rest of his life following his wife around shopping centers. It's ridiculous.

When you live on a boat you're exposed to hundreds of strangers every month. With boating as the common interest, you soon learn what a man did before retirement and how he views life since retirement. And the more retired couples you talk to the more you come to realize that retirement, as it is viewed by most people, is a snare and a delusion. The best thing that could happen to a person is to be forced to continue to work. There should be a law prohibiting retirement.

I decided early on that I never wanted to find myself in a position where I didn't have to do some kind of work to provide Dory and me with a decent existence. I'd spent enough time in retirement towns across the Sun Belt to know that having nothing to do from morning to night except play a little golf, take a little nap, do a little reading, watch a little TV, play a little pinochle with the neighbors, drink a little too much, and slip a little farther into senility was not my idea of enjoying one's golden years. That kind of retirement is nothing more than a withdrawal from life, with the ultimate withdrawal coming the day they plant you in the ground or scatter your ashes at sea.

I'm not saying that a man doesn't deserve a change of pace and a lessening of tension and stress after reaching sixty-five. What I am trying to point out is that the change of pace doesn't have to be a panic stop. Why, we treat horses better than we treat people in this country. When a horse finishes a race they walk him around to let him gradually cool off. If he's been a winning horse, they keep him busy siring colts with some of the qualities that made him a winner in the first place. Now, before you fellows get the notion that I am about to recommend that you retire to some sort of breeding farm (not necessarily a bad idea), hear me out.

I think that when a man reaches fifty-five he should start training for his life between the ages of sixty-five and seventy-five. If he works for a large corporation, on retirement he might be put on a two-days-a-week consulting basis with definite assignments that a younger man couldn't handle because of lack of experience. Or he should be trained to work in a field that has always interested him but he hadn't had the time to become involved with during his overactive years. The fact that a man has held a responsible position up to a certain date shouldn't mean that he has lost his faculties or ability to make decisions the following day.

The thrill of living is getting up in the morning, knowing that you have more enjoyable projects than time will allow. It's enjoying a blend of work and play. It's collapsing in a chair at 5:00 P.M., totally pooped from having been busy achieving worthwhile objectives that *mean* something to somebody.

But just the opposite happens to the great majority of people who reach sixty-five. They're forced to stand aside to allow younger people to come along. Well, who made that rule? Certainly not the people approaching sixty-five. Most of them don't want to stand aside. They'd much prefer to keep working, but maybe at a slower pace. And as for giving the young a break, screw 'em. Let them bust their picks trying to get where you already are. Whoever said life was easy? Not the man who's reached the top the hard way. And now that he's on top he isn't anxious to graciously step aside. And I don't blame him.

I got to thinking about all of this when I woke up this morning. I was lying in bed, staring at the ceiling when Dory kissed me and asked, "Do you have a lot to do today?" As it turned out I did. For one thing I had about four football games to watch. But I also had a column idea I wanted to work on plus I had a marine-industry newsletter to put together and I had six or seven letters to write to people wanting to take part in our European cruise and there were two short articles to be written for a Dutch newspaper. Yes, I had a lot to do. And I was grateful for the opportunity to make an attempt to do at least some of them.

You see, I've been very lucky. Whenever I've worked for a big company and have almost reached the top, I've been fired. When my advertising-agency business would almost reach the point where more personnel were needed, Dory would say, "Let's start taking long weekends instead of making more money." When I hit forty-five, Dory agreed with my suggestion that we take a year off and race our sailboat. When I reached fifty-five and was on the verge of becoming a "big" advertising agency, Dory suggested we chuck it all and live on a boat in Florida. When I celebrated my sixtieth birthday I was offered a chance to write a column, and a whole new career opened up for me. At sixty-five I sold the magazine on having me publish a marine-industry newsletter for them, another career switch.

Shortly after my sixty-sixth birthday, I found myself putting together a tour of European canals for readers of *Motor Boating and Sailing* magazine. Another new and exciting career to add to the collection. The only difference I've found from my pre-senior-citizen days is that I can get into a movie theater for half price. Other than that, I'm up to my ass in enjoyable, satisfying, ego-fulfilling work. Not that my life is perfect, because it isn't. I've got a health problem that could cut my budding careers short. But then, so could a truck on I-95. I have just barely enough money to live a pretty idyllic life, but the need to keep humping is always there . . . and always will be, with luck.

But life wasn't meant to be perfect. If we didn't have the lows we wouldn't appreciate the highs. And when I hear somebody my age complaining about getting old, I shake my head in wonderment. You see, I'm not getting older, I'm getting better. I'm expecting to reach my peak in a couple of years.

One more thing. Last night a young gal asked Dory what *she* did to keep her mind occupied. Dory told her she worked on our boat and read a lot and helped me with my many projects.

"Yes," the girl persisted, "but what does your *life* consist of?"

Dory said, "Dick is my life. I live for him."

The young gal, having spent the previous half hour extolling the virtues of ERA and Women's Lib, said, "Oh." She wasn't impressed. How could she be? It's going to take her another forty years to learn what life's all about.

But Dory's words of wisdom made me realize that this year's resolution should be to beat the unbeatable foe. Not so that I can achieve all of my goals and complete my projects and enjoy my multicareers. They're important to me, of course. But they're only the frosting on the cake compared to my primary reason for living. That reason is a simple four-letter word . . . Dory. Thank God government hasn't encroached into our lives to the point where it can force us to retire from marriage and loving at age sixty-five.

If it's true that "Life Begins at Forty" then it must be true that "living" begins anew every day from the day you reach sixty-five. Enjoy, all you about-to-be senior citizens.

The best is yet to come!

· S I X ·

Sage Advice

Confessions of an Ex-Yacht Broker

⚓ *APRIL, 1980*

Government surveys reveal a surprising statistic: More than 93 percent of boat owners living north of the Mason-Dixon Line say they plan to move to Florida upon retiring and become yacht brokers. They give as reasons for this decision the fact that a yacht broker appears to be a person who spends most of his time sipping gin and tonics on the poop deck of a luxurious yacht, while millionaires stuff thousand-dollar bills in his pocket. Lest you count yourself among these misguided souls, let me set you straight. Being a successful yacht broker requires hard work and real knowledge.

I, too, once harbored dreams of finding a pot of gold at the end of a yacht-broker's rainbow. Today, I am a wiser man. I'd be a lot poorer if Lady Luck hadn't favored me with a smile along the way. And I'd be a broken man had my wife not tossed my business cards in the drink, torn the phone out of the wall, and canceled my trust account at the local bank. But during the ninety days I spent as a yacht broker, I learned about the yacht-broker's life . . . the hard way.

Being a successful yacht broker
requires hard work and real knowledge.

I am by nature a lethargic person. I never stand if I can sit, sit if I can lie down, stay awake if I can nap, or walk if I can drive. My idea of labor is to sit at the typewriter, virtually motionless, and let my fingers do the walking. About a year ago I did an ad for a friend of mine who had a large yacht for sale in Fort Lauderdale. When the ad appeared, my phone number was listed because there was no phone on the man's boat. Before the ad appeared in the magazine, however, the boat was sold. So, I had to tell interested parties the yacht was no longer on the market. Most people simply muttered something like "ship!" and hung up. But one fellow was more persistent.

"What other yachts do you have listed?" he asked.

"None," I replied. "I'm not a yacht broker. I simply wrote the ad."

"Well, can you find me a boat like the one in the ad?" he asked.

My inclination was to say no, but my greedy nature took over and I found myself saying, "Well, as long as you understand I am not a yacht broker, I'll see what I can do."

A few weeks later I found myself looking at a twenty-three-thousand-dollar commission check and thinking, "Wow, at this rate I can make two hundred fifty thousand dollars a year and only work a few hours a week." Boy, was I ever wrong about that.

For the next three or four months I lived the imagined life of a yacht broker, sitting for hours watching the phone and waiting for it to ring; racing like mad from wherever I was to reach the phone on those occasions when it did ring; stuttering and stammering while searching frantically through piles of disorganized files for a boat that would match the needs of the person on the phone; driving for hours seeking boats for people who didn't know what they wanted and couldn't afford it if they found it; suffering leg cramps and bruises and skinned shins and aching backs from having climbed on and around and off hundreds of boats that didn't resemble their owners' descriptions, weren't worth half of what the owners wanted, and wouldn't pass even the minimum survey by a near-blind inexperienced surveyor who did his business by mail.

Meanwhile, money was pouring out for advertising, gas, entertaining free-loading clients, licenses, phone bills, and a hundred other little bits and pieces I hadn't figured on. And I began to think about a bit of advice a friend had given me shortly after making my big sale. "Retire," he said. "This may be the only sale you'll ever make. Get out while you're ahead." It began to appear as though he were right. But each time I'd think about taking down my shingle, something inside me would say, "Give it one more week. Maybe that nutty doctor will buy that boat you showed him and you'll make enough to cover your expenses." So, I kept hanging in there, getting more nervous and tense by the day. I was popping Valiums like peanuts, taking sleeping pills nightly, and seriously considering seeing a shrink. I was, as the kids say, strung out.

I began to wonder why anyone would want to be a yacht broker. I wasn't having any fun. I wasn't spending time sipping cocktails on million-dollar yachts. I wasn't deeply tanned from sailing on sea trials. I was sort of a putty-green color from sitting in my office all day, I had developed a nervous twitch in one eye, my heart fluttered constantly, I developed a strange lurch to my walk, and there was an ominous ache in my gut twenty-four hours a day. I've since been advised I was suffering from Yacht Broker's syndrome. All in all, this felt like work.

I began to think about the real yacht brokers—pros who appeared to be calm, cool, relaxed, and happy. They were all normal and successful and. . . . Ah, I thought, that's the key word: "successful." They'd been in the business long enough and they'd worked hard enough to have become successful. But had they gone through the miseries I was suffering when they started? I determined to find out.

My survey revealed some interesting facts. One man said, "You have to develop a fatalistic attitude. When the phone rings you must not allow your hopes to rise. Assume it is your ex-wife calling to remind you about your alimony payments. Then if it turns out to be a prospect, you're pleasantly surprised. When a man says he wants to see a ninety-foot, three-masted schooner, resign youself to the fact that he'll probably end up buying a run-down, twenty-eight-foot houseboat. But show him the ninety-footer because he may just be for real."

Another said, "I've been in this business for so long I don't think about it once I leave the office. I just go home, make a triple martini, and grub in the garden. If it's been a good day I plant some flowers. If it's been a bad day I take an ax and strike out at whatever is within reach. You'd be amazed at how much pressure can be eased by a few moments of destruction and drunkenness."

A third said, "When I get a prospect in the office who says he's looking for a really big, expensive yacht, I pull something out of the files that is over one hundred feet and is located a couple of hundred miles away. Then I tell him my car is in the shop for repairs and ask if he would mind driving his car. If he hesitates, I write him off as a phony. But if he offers to fly me there in his private jet, I start looking for listings seriously."

I was told by one broker, "It helps your state of mind if you are very, very rich. That way, you can tell yourself, 'If I sell this guy a boat I'll be in a higher tax bracket and it will actually cost me money.' That way, you can really become ambivalent toward the outcome. The trouble is, this attitude drives buyers nuts and they frequently will buy just to put the broker down."

The solution to my problem came about the same way most of my problems have been solved during the past forty years. I began to eat and drink too much, lose too much sleep, look too haggard, act too edgy, and lose my sense of humor. My wife mentioned a few of the above flaws on numerous occasions and my answer always was, "Look, it comes with the territory. What do you want me to do? Give up? I have too much pride to do that."

One day she strode into my office, poured my martini over my head, threw my box of business cards out the porthole, and tore the phone out of the wall.

"Wait a minute," I protested. "You've just taken away my tools."

"Face it," she replied, "you're not a real yacht broker. You were just lucky. What you are is a writer and ne'er-do-well. Or, as my father used to describe you, a born bum. Now, get your feet off the desk and help me cart these files to the dumpster."

Today I'm eating and drinking less but sleeping more. I frequently refuse to answer the phone. Today I'm off on another tangent for which I am equally ill-suited. But that's another story.

On Friendship

⚓ *MARCH, 1979*

Whenever people ask me if the cruising life I lead doesn't cause me to lose a lot of my friends, I'm reminded of the story told about the late John Barrymore. It seems Barrymore was wandering down Broadway hoping to run into a pal to join him in a drink when he spotted a fellow tippler hurrying past. Grabbing the man by the arm, he suggested they repair to the nearest bar for a snort, but was told this was impossible. It seems his drinking buddy was on his way to see a friend.

"A friend?" asked Barrymore. "Let me come along. I've always wanted to see one."

Now, if that sounds a bit cynical even for an old curmudgeon like me, forgive me. But it does illustrate a point, which is that too many of us tend to look on casual acquaintances as life-long friends without whom we could not survive. And this fear of leaving these so-called friends deters millions of people from breaking away from the old neighborhood and seeking new adventures and meeting new people who, given a chance, might become real friends. The truth is, your best friend may be someone you've known all your life or he might be the person you were introduced to last night. Most of us tend to think of friends as being people with familiar faces. While I'm not as cynical as old John Barrymore, I tend to think of people with familiar faces as being people with familiar faces. I don't confuse them with those rare and wonderful creatures I call friends.

I was reminded of this last Thanksgiving when a group of us sat around a picnic table set up alongside our boat, *Simba*, which is moored on Fort Lauderdale's New River. It was a glorious day and seated at the table, gorging themselves on turkey and fixings, were Bill and Patsy Bolling, whom we had met only six months ago but who qualify as being the best of friends; Charlie Thomas, a friend of some fifteen years standing and considered as a part of the family; our younger daughter, Linda, with whom we have a relationship which transcends the normal parents-daughter pattern; our granddaughter, Chelsea; and the Bollings' son, Billy, and his woman friend.

The day before we'd gotten a call from another dear friend, Dave Olson, who now lives in Denver and the day prior to that we'd received a long letter from our good buddy Fritz Seyfarth, now snugged down in Man-O'-War Cay in the Abacos. That same day I'd talked to another person who more than qualifies as a friend, Jeff Hammond, and failed in my efforts to lure him into piling his family on a plane to join us dockside for the feast. Along with a few other good people, including my older daughter, Barbara, my friendship roster is pretty well filled out.

Thanks to the eight trips we've made along the Intracoastal Waterway, our two America's Cup summers in Newport, and the folks who read this column, there is seldom a day goes by without someone stopping me to say hello or slowing down as they go by *Simba* to holler "Hey, Bradley! How yuh doin'?" Some of these friendly and familiar faces may someday become friends. Who knows? The world of boating is small and closely knit and the longer we're a part of it the more aware we become of how interwoven the relationships can become.

The wonderful thing about boating is that people of totally differing backgrounds and personalities can meet and become fast friends and cruising companions because of this common interest. For example, last year at Man-O'-War Cay we met a retired university professor and a retired bakery owner who developed an interest in sailing at the same time, bought cruising sailboats within weeks of one another, and who recently completed a successful cruise to the Virgin Islands in tandem. Without boating as the basis for their friendship, these two might never have progressed beyond a nodding acquaintanceship. Now each can honestly say he has a friend.

I have said several times in the past that one of the great things about boating is that moving around prevents others from learning how rotten a human being you really are. Your wife and kids know the awful truth, but they're stuck with you. The boating world sees only that friendly guy who pours drinks freely and spins sea stories by the hour. Before you've run through your entire string of tall tales, either they've moved on to newer waters or you have. In either case, your secret is safe.

But the couple who stay in the next slip to you all winter, putting up with your mooching of drinks, your boring war stories, your screaming tirades with the little woman, your yapping dog who never really has learned to wait until he gets to the end of the dock before relieving himself, your VHF radio blasting away at all hours, and your habit of cluttering the dock with oil cans, tools, fenders, dinghies, and other menaces to onshore navigation . . . they can be considered friends.

As far as I am aware, Dory and I have never "lost" a friend. There are some we haven't seen in ten years, others with whom we have spoken only twice in several years, a few with whom we exchange letters on a semiannual basis, and hundreds of names and faces that form a blurry image of places and events long forgotten. But our real friends are always with us where it counts . . . in our hearts and in our thoughts.

Cruising is a bit like cleaning out an old attic. You get rid of a lot of stuff you don't really like, keep a few cherished items, and determine to be a lot more choosy in the future. I just hope you're as lucky as Dory and I have been during the past twenty years of boating when it comes to friends.

Because there's nothing in the world so satisfying as being able to start out a story with the words, "I have a good friend who . . ."

Working Hard and Enjoying It More

⚓ *FEBRUARY, 1980*

To thousands of boat owners, the American Dream is to retire aboard a comfortable cruising boat and flee to some sun-drenched island in the Caribbean.

To other thousands, those who have achieved what they thought was the American Dream, retirement afloat has turned into an ever more frightening nightmare. They have watched inflation shatter the dream and turn their once-serene lives into a day-to-day battle to keep from sinking in the quicksand of bankruptcy.

It's one thing to read about the ravages of inflation and quite something else to see it happen to your friends and neighbors. It is sickening to watch a man's face change over a period of months from joy and contentment to fear and pressure. Few couples are prepared to augment their incomes by stepping back into working environments. Some cannot bring themselves to return to a daily job, while others are not equipped, because of health or lack of expertise, to find employment.

While it is tougher on retirees, young couples who have dropped out for a few years also find their plans disrupted because of the cost of living. Oddly enough, young people frequently have more difficulty adjusting to the situation than older folks. Perhaps the older one gets, the more one accepts the cruel fact that there is no such thing as security. Not as long as one is alive and full of the juices of living. But even knowing that, it is hard not to turn bitter when plans laid and lovingly built over the years go astray because of skyrocketing living costs.

We have a very dear friend who retired ten years ago and moved aboard a beautiful ketch with traditional lines and ample accommodations for a bachelor. All went well for several years as our friend took his boat north and south with the seasons. Then inflation reared its ugly head, while stock dividends fell off. As might be expected, each year sees his position eroded until the sale of his lovely yacht has become a necessity. When it goes, so goes his life-style and much of the reason for getting up in the morning. Fortunately, this particular fellow is able to view the situation realistically and even optimistically. But it is still a tragedy.

Other couples we know have sold property acquired over a period of years, planning to live on the monthly payments. But increased costs of living combined with lapses of income have forced these couples to scurry around in search of part-time jobs, or to return to their home towns to reclaim property. In either case, their dreams were shattered.

Because I make my living with my fingers, inflation hasn't hit me as hard as it has others. I've been performing on the high wire without a net for so long that I wouldn't know how to handle security as most people my age think of it. In fact, my *modus operandi* has been to deliberately avoid security all of my life for fear that I might come to enjoy it. I've been in the pool with the sharks for so long that a recession will just be business as usual. In fact, I suspect I derive a certain satisfaction out of being forced to scamper around and compete with someone half my age. When friends tell me my life-style keeps me young, I assure them it's because I can't afford to get old.

I've noticed that other couples seem to fall into the same category. They're either hustling and happy, or inactive and vaguely discontent. Strangely enough, the fully retired couples envy those who are forced to keep busy, while those who are busy haven't time to envy anybody. If this sounds as though I'm advocating poverty, I'm not. What I am advocating is keeping busy.

An example of what I have just been talking about is a couple named Bob and Annette, who live on a small sailboat that is their first boat ever. They decided one day that it was time to try something new. They sold their property in Kentucky, gave their horses away to friends, and drove to Florida. After looking around the docks for a few days, they settled on a thirty-five-foot sailboat that would be perfect for a pair of twenty-five-year-old newlyweds but isn't what I would recommend for a middle-aged couple.

But they are the happiest people I've ever met. They are joyous, truly joyous, from morning to night. When inflation forced them to augment their income, he hustled off and found a job working in a marine supply store where he could learn about boats quickly. She got a real-estate license and every morning they go their respective ways, wearing big smiles and waving a cheery good morning to everyone on the docks. At night, when they return, their smiles are as big as ever and they exude happiness and fun. Two minutes later they are seated in their cockpit sipping cocktails and munching popcorn. Tell me they're suffering? No way!

The "good life" envisioned by most people just isn't everybody's thing. I came back from six months in the Bahamas suffering from hypertension for the first time in my life. I thought I was relaxed and having a ball. Actually, I was frustrated and concerned about my work and communication foul-ups and bank balances. Obviously, retirement is not for me.

When I meet men my own age who spend their days contemplating their navels or shopping with their wives or playing gin rummy with other old codgers, I depart the scene as quickly as I can. I like to be around people who are alive and vital and young in spirit.

When people say to me, "Aren't you a little old to be starting yet another career?" I think about fellows like Bob Hope who, at the ripe age of eighty, is still going strong.

And when I really wonder if I'm going crazy to be so busy, I recall what eighty-seven-year-old George Burns said recently. When asked how long he thought he would live, he replied, "I can't die. I'm booked through 1985."

Life's Stolen Moments

⚓ *MARCH, 1982*

"Life's most precious moments are the moments you steal." I don't know the origin of that bit of philosophy, but I got it from Ash Bown, the San Diego sailing genius who taught Dennis Conner port from starboard. Ash has owned an ancient forty-foot Owens Cutter for as long as anyone can remember and has been a member of the San Diego Yacht Club equally as long. Like many boat owners, Ash would drop down to the club every morning and evening on his way to and from work to make a minor adjustment in his dock lines or simply stare up at the rigging in search of a potential problem. Actually, Ash just liked to stand there and admire his beloved yacht. It was during a morning period such as I have just described when Ash spoke those words of wisdom. I have remembered them for the past twenty years.

Dory and I stole a year and a half back in 1961 to go racing on our beautiful Finnish-built Eight-Meter *Cheerio*. I walked away from a very comfortable income to concentrate on making *Cheerio* go fast around the race course off San Diego. We shouldn't have taken the time and gone into debt for such a frivolous purpose, by all the standards of good judgment and conformity. But we had one hell of a great time, won a lot of races (including the 1962 Ensenada Race against some 350 boats), and managed to beat, at one time or another, many of the great names of sailboat racing including Lowell North, Jerry Driscoll, Bill Ficker, and Jim Kilroy (on his original *Kialoa*). It was the most exciting eighteen months we have ever enjoyed and we wouldn't sell it back for a million dollars. Actually, it was kind of fun being pointed out as the only yachtsman in southern California to be campaigning a fifty-foot racing sloop while collecting unemployment insurance.

I have another old friend from San Diego who has developed his own philosophy. Fritz Seyfarth wrote me not long ago to defend himself against my charge of not wanting to work.

"Work," Fritz wrote, "is something someone says I must do and who pays me for doing it. Work generally requires performing some distasteful service. Projects, on the other hand, are things I do because I want to do them. They're projects of my choosing. And while both require effort, it boils down to a matter of values. I try to minimize 'work' and maximize 'projects.' Unfortunately, this philosophy often leads to a state of abject poverty. The down side of poverty is having to watch my lovely old ketch suffer from a lack of yard maintenance and being required to spend a good part of my golden years pumping the old girl out."

It should be noted that Fritz spends his time in the Virgin Islands, anchored off lovely islands and pounding away on his typewriter when he isn't pumping. His latest report revealed that he reduced his pumping from a hundred strokes an hour to only five after buying a gigantic pump. Fritz has all the qualities of an ornery mule. When he makes up his mind to do something, he pursues his goal in the face of adverse winds and tides until Mother Nature either wins or gives up in disgust. Fritz never gives up.

"I could sell more of my work if only I could write flattering letters to editors, but I can't bring myself to do that," he says. "I could take a good-paying job for a couple of years and build up a kitty but I don't want to give up my freedom. The perfect solution would be to marry a beautiful young lady with lots of money, but the only offers I have had come from aging gay fellows in Lily Pulitzer pink-and-green outfits, or native women with five kids. But I have to admit I'm getting awfully tired of eating seaweed."

His fear of losing his freedom made me wonder if all his "projecting" wasn't a form of captivity. He accuses me of being a captive to my material needs, and he's right in some degree. My profligate life-style in years past forces me to keep my fingers to the typewriter just to pay for bits and pieces of materialism that have long since worn out or been tossed away. So, neither of us is truly free but we both enjoy our captivity to a certain extent and make the best of it.

A philosopher I once worked with described freedom as "having the opportunity to set your own objectives, make your own decisions, and take full responsibility for the outcome of those decisions." That's always been good enough for me and I have done my damnedest to achieve that particular form of freedom. As for finding total freedom, I just don't know. Florida is filling up with people who have worked all their lives to accumulate enough money to live where they want to live and do what they want to do when they want to do it. The problem is, they have forgotten what it is they wanted to do. They have no opportunities to steal a precious moment because all of their moments are open and empty.

I suppose the point of all this is to encourage those of you who can't see a time ahead when you will have enough money to chuck it all and just spend your days doing nothing. If you are still hustling for a buck when you are eighty-five, you'll be one of the lucky ones. If you're fortunate enough to be able to make a comfortable living with projects that bring you satisfaction as well as money, count your blessings. If, God forbid, you are loaded with ill-gotten gains and don't *really* have to work to make ends meet, there is only one sensible answer.

Buy an old boat, preferably wood. Take it to Florida and park it in a pleasant marina. (Good luck with that search. Nice places to keep a boat in Florida are getting harder and harder to find.) From the day you buy her until the day they lay either the boat or you to rest, you won't have a spare moment. Between the heat and humidity and the daily showers, you'll be fighting dry rot and flaking varnish and peeling paint. The days, weeks, months, and years will race by, broken only by rare moments when you sit under the shade of your bimini and sip a cold beer with a friend. By the time your wife calls you for lunch you'll be ready. When the tinkle of ice in a cold glass tells you it's cocktail time, you'll think you've just been reprieved from Death Row. While your neighbors are preparing themselves for an early grave, griping and grumbling about minor irritations, you'll be vital and alive and full of life.

Oh, there'll be times when you feel like selling that damned boat and taking up golf. But don't do it. Because every night just before you hit the sack you can walk down to the dock to look at that beautiful old hulk as she rides quietly at her slip. And when your wife calls out, "Harry, when you're through looking at that dumb old boat, will you please put some food out for the cat?" you can smile and answer, "Yes, dear," knowing that you have just stolen one of life's most precious moments.

"Compromise" Is a Dirty Word

⚓ *MAY, 1978*

If you're looking forward to the day when you can move aboard a boat and live a more simplified existence, let me give you a word of warning. Living aboard *can* be an inexpensive, interesting, and stimulating way of life *providing* both you and your mate agree on a mutually satisfying level of simplicity. If either one of you is forced to drop below that level, your whole program is in trouble from the start.

Generally speaking, men suffer more pressures, frustrations, and harassments during their business careers than their wives put up with during the same period. Thus, when a man dreams of getting away from it all and living a simpler life-style, he's apt to create a vision of Robinson Crusoe. Sailing off to a remote island in the sun aboard a twenty-six-foot sailboat with no engine, no head other than a wooden bucket, no lights, a kerosene stove, and no refrigerator can be appealing to a man who's had it up to here with complications.

His wife, on the other hand, may think of living aboard as lounging on the aft deck of a fifty-foot power cruiser, the washer/dryer churning away belowdecks, a pie cooking in her microwave oven, and her husband busy cleaning the main saloon with the built-in vacuum-cleaner system. A pair of bright yellow electric cords run from the boat to the dock and if she tires of watching the action onshore she can turn on the television. She's perfectly willing to go along with her husband's foolishness about living on a boat, but she's not about to become Tarzan's mate at this stage of her life.

While this might seem to be an insolvable problem, with patience and flexibility on both sides a workable solution can be achieved. Through compromise, each party can satisfy his or her basic needs and achieve a level of simplicity that both can live with.

Unfortunately, many men fail to describe in detail the kind of existence they hope to live when retirement arrives. You can imagine the wife's shock when she gets her first look at the cramped and tippy little teacup her husband introduces as "your new home afloat." Her reaction is usually violent, negative, and inflexible. His counterreaction is then violent, affirmative, and equally inflexible. This is called a Mexican Standoff.

Most often the deadlock is broken in one of two ways. Either the couple retires to the old homestead and a life of boredom or the husband gets his way and they take off on an ill-fated cruise that is short, stormy, and destructive to the marriage. It doesn't have to happen.

Let me give you three examples, each of them concerning actual couples, which will help to guide you through the reefs of purchasing your dream boat for your autumn years.

Don and Holly tried living aboard a forty-three-foot sailboat that provided them with luxury accommodations, but was more boat than they could handle under sail. When the time came to find a smaller boat, each listed his or her requirements for a minimum level of simplicity. It turned out that both detested just two facets of cruising in the Bahamas. Sleepless nights due to bugs and/or excessive heat and humidity and warm drinks. By adding a gasoline generator and a small freezer, they now sleep under blankets year-round and enjoy cold beer and iced beverages while their neighbors accuse them of being hedonists. They complicated their lives just a little to gain a beautiful and simple life-style.

At the opposite end of the spectrum we have Bill and Dorothy, who owned and operated a luxurious sixty-three-foot sailboat for charter in the Virgin Islands for some years. When they tired of this life, they set about to design a boat that would provide them with a simple life-style but with those luxury items each felt was necessary to enjoy living aboard to the fullest. They ended up with a fifty-foot custom trawler that sleeps two in utmost comfort, gives Bill the three-thousand-mile cruising range he wanted plus his impressive high-fidelity system, while she has her electric galley, microwave oven, and washer/dryer combination that is served by an eight-hundred-gallon water capacity. Obviously, their level of simplicity is far above Don and Holly's, but both couples enjoy their boats equally.

Our third example, a couple whom we shall call Fred and Myrtle, followed the customary approach to moving aboard. Fred hoped to re-create his youth by sailing a thirty-nine-foot sloop through the islands. Myrtle wasn't much for the liveaboard life under the best of circumstances, and sharing the cramped quarters of a sailboat was not her idea of fun afloat. But Fred wasn't the type to be swayed by his wife's objections. Like a dutiful wife, Myrtle gave in but silently swore to have her way in the long ... or short ... run. Fred had plans to cruise for ten years minimum. Myrtle told her friends she figured it would take her two years to do him in, figuratively speaking. Do you have any doubts as to the end of the story?

Last December, almost two years to the day, Fred and Myrtle left the anchorage in Man-O'-War in the Bahamas and headed for their newly purchased condominium overlooking the Waterway in Florida. The boat has been listed for sale and Fred's boating days have ended. From now on he will bore the bunch around the shuffleboard courts with stories of his cruising days in the islands. Poor Fred will never understand what went wrong. It will never occur to him that if he had compromised and given his wife an environment which satisfied both of them, instead of just him, he'd still be enjoying a simple and satisfying way of life in the Bahamas. But to a fellow like Fred, "compromise" is a dirty word.

On the day Fred and Myrtle sailed off, a friend of mine rowed over to bid them good-bye. During the conversation, Fred looked over at Bill's comfortable trawler and said, "I sure hope I never get so old I have to go to power-boating."

He won't. I predict he'll be dead by Christmas, possibly the victim of a hit-and-run old lady pushing a shopping cart in a Vero Beach supermarket.

On his headstone should be the words, "Here Lies Fred, Recalled by Maker Due to a Deficiency in Judgment."

Running Scared

⚓ *MARCH, 1981*

"I'm selling my boat, buying a farm in the mountains of Tennessee, stocking it with freeze-dry foods, putting in a good-sized garden, buying some pigs and cattle, and when the bottom drops out of the dollar and everyone's starving, I'll be in fat city. And if anyone comes around to take it away from me, I'll have all the guns and ammo I need to wipe 'em off the face of the earth."

Does that sound farfetched? It isn't. I have met any number of people who are doing just that. Getting ready for the end of the world as we know it. Every day new books are published and new newsletters appear that warn of the coming disaster. "Buy gold! Buy silver!" "Run for the hills!" "Get a horse!" "Don't take any wooden nickels!" "Get ready to ward off those minority groups!" "*They* are coming for you! Be ready to kill *them* before they kill you!"

If they really believe in all that, how come they charge so much for their newsletters? I mean, if our money isn't going to be worth a damn, why do they need so much of it? If they are really concerned about our future, why don't they just give that information away? Or why don't they ask you to pay for your newsletter subscription with a pig or cow? Or maybe a thousand rounds of ammo? But no, they say, "Send me fifty or a hundred dollars and I'll tell you what is going to happen. I'll scare the living bejeezus out of you and get rich doing it. I'll quote the Bible and the *Farmer's Almanac* and prove to you that the United States cannot survive four years of anybody."

I've been assured by friends who make a study of such things that Social Security will be broke in a few years, the dollar won't be worth a penny, mobs will roam the streets searching for food, the government will be in disarray, the Russians will be bombing us, millions will die, and the only survivors will be on their little farms tucked away in the mountains. My attitude is, if that's all that's going to happen, what

The only survivors will be tucked
away in their little farms in the mountains.

is all the fuss about? I've seen all that happen already. Well, not all of it. But part of it. And we're all still here.

What puzzles me are the people who are selling their boats to buy farms. I'd be doing just the opposite. If I were starving in the inner city of New York or Chicago or Miami, the first place I would head would be for the country, where all those people have hoarded all that food and where all those fat little pigs and plump cattle are standing around just waiting to be slaughtered and butchered and eaten. I'd keep in mind what the old bank robber Willie Sutton was supposed to have said when he was asked why he robbed banks. His answer was, "Cause that's where the money is." Well, those disenfranchised folks from the burned-out sections of the city will have enough street smarts to know that when you are starving and you have a gun and a car, you go where the food is and you take what you need.

Man, it's going to be downright *crowded* out there in the country! I, for one, don't plan to be here, that's for sure. But I don't want to be out on the farm, either. What's left? Well, how about a few thousand islands out there in a blue sea? How about a few million square miles of clean ocean with enough fish to keep us alive and healthy until things settle down back home? How about clean water that comes from the skies? How about dropping anchor in a quiet cove where you know you're not going to see a carload of screaming freaks roaring over your fields, chasing your cows and pigs.

No sir, that farm stuff sure isn't my style. For one thing, I don't believe it will happen. I don't think God would be so mean as to do something like that just when I've started to collect my Social Security. I don't think the greedy bloodsuckers in Washington will allow anything to interfere with that easy life they have. Can you imagine those congressmen and senators, almost all of whom are attorneys, letting something happen that would mean they'd have to work for their livelihood? No way! It'll never happen.

But in the meantime, my friends who have moved to the mountains are going to be sitting on their front porches, just a-rocking away and chewing tobacky and talking about crops and the weather and the subsidies and the neighbor-folk. Damn! That's my idea of death on the lay-away plan. I sure as hell don't want to end my days wearing overalls and a straw hat and scraping cow dung off my shoes. I've seen hillbillies and I don't have a yen to call them "neighbor," thank you. Not that they aren't good folks, God-fearing, and all that. But when someone starts telling me about the joys of that kind of life I get a picture of Billy Carter in my mind and I say, "If it's a choice of starving or having someone like him for a neighbor, I'll take my chances with a yellow feather. Or a worm and a cane pole, for that matter."

I keep getting another picture in my mind. It's a penthouse in New York and there's Howard Ruff and Harry Browne and all those doom-sayers sitting around a marble cocktail table in their underwear, drunk as skunks, and laughing till they weep. There are scantily clad beautiful women serving drinks and lighting the men's big fat cigars. The phone rings every few minutes and one of them picks it up and gets a big smile on his face. When he puts it down, he turns to the others and says, "It's working, boys, just like I said it would. Our real-estate company has just sold another hundred farms up in that rocky area just outside of Ashville. And our cattle company is selling cows like they were going out of style. And pigs? Man, we got pigs going out the door like you wouldn't believe."

Then Howard turns to Harry and says, "Did you really think when we started this scam that so many people would believe it?"

And Harry says, "I just keep remembering what that guy used to say, 'There's a sucker born every minute!' "

So the third guy in the group says, "Well, I figure we can start dumping silver and gold in about ten days. When that happens each of us will be worth three billion dollars. Good old American dollars. How sweet it is!"

After each dream I get up and look at my boat and say, "I'm sticking with you, old girl. And when our friends are dying of boredom up there in Dullsville, North Carolina, or wherever, we'll be living it up right here at the dock. And with the price of beef and pork dropping so fast, I think we'll have sirloin steaks smothered in pork chops and lean bacon for dinner every night from now on."

Good night, Howard. Good night, Harry. You're a barrel of laughs. The problem is, you don't know it.

Sage Advice

⚓ *JANUARY, 1983*

"No matter how wealthy you become, you'll never have enough money to buy back the weekends lost working."

That profound bit of advice was given me by a friend of mine, Bill Short, some twenty years ago. Bill was an avid yachtsman and owned at the time Humphrey Bogart's old boat, *Santana.* He operated his own business and knew how easy it was to fall into the trap of working on weekends to catch up on paperwork. I never forgot his advice and I follow it to this day, even though my "work" consists of sitting at a typewriter. When I heard that Bill had died many years before his time, I was glad to know that he had taken his weekends and used them to enjoy his yacht.

It's been my experience that most people could accomplish an average week's work in about three days if left to their own devices. But most of us are trained over the years to put in a specific number of hours each week, and we manage to stretch out our three days of accomplishment to five days. Part of this is due to the fact that much of our work consists of needless red tape or non-essential trivia or record-keeping. As time goes by, more space is needed for old records, and so larger quarters are rented and more file cabinets are purchased to house the worthless records. Then more people are required to keep track of the records and . . . well, you get the drift.

During my thirty years as an advertising-agency owner, I tried to reduce clutter to a minimum. I finally reached a point where I didn't make carbons of letters, on the basis that *I* knew what I had said and the client knew what I'd said and, besides, I knew the client would file my letter and I could always call and have his secretary read it to me. It worked like a charm. I also went for the same number of years without business cards. I knew that the easiest brush-off in the world is, "Give me your card and I'll get back to you." But I would say, "I don't have a card with me so I'll call you next week."

During those years my boat was never more than fifteen minutes away, and I found myself stretching my weekends by leaving my office at noon on Friday and getting back at noon on Monday. Eventually, I closed the office about 3:00 P.M. on Thursday afternoon and got back about noon on Tuesday. But on stormy weekends I found myself sorely tempted to "run by the office" just to put in a few hours' work. Those were the times when Bill Short's sage advice steered me straight.

During my recent stay in New York I discovered an interesting fact about my working habits. I went into the *Motor Boating and Sailing* office almost every day. I was given an office and a typewriter and encouraged to knock out a column or two. During my five weeks in the office I managed to turn out about five hours of productive writing because the environment was wrong for me. I am accustomed to working in my own little office with the only sound being that of music coming from my stereo system. But in New York there were so many distractions that I got virtually no work done. There was always someone wandering by for a chat or I was wandering to their offices for a chat or I found myself eavesdropping on conversations in nearby offices (the walls are only six feet high and you can hear five conversations at once).

Finally, out of frustration, I told Dory I was planning to go into the office on Saturdays to get something accomplished. But she had the good judgment to remind me of Bill Short's old rule and we went walking instead.

Oddly enough, when we got back to Faro Blanco I found myself seated at my typewriter within thirty minutes, grinding out a column and happy as a clam to be back in my floating cubbyhole aboard *Simba*. But as much as I enjoyed my working environment and had a whole pile of work before me, when Friday evening arrived I shut off my typewriter and didn't touch it again until Monday morning. This didn't please Dory because I had papers scattered everywhere and she prefers to keep *Simba* neat and clutter-free.

Each time that she carefully picked her way through the mess I'd made, she'd grumble about husbands who didn't have an office or regular working hours. She'd encourage me to spend a few hours on Saturday or Sunday finishing up some of the work I'd started so she could clear a path through the debris. But I resisted her suggestions and reminded her of Bill Short's advice.

"Dory, a wise man told me many years ago that no matter how wealthy I became, I would never have enough money to buy back my lost weekends."

Her answer was typical of her approach to life. "Look, I'm not asking you to buy back lost weekends. I only wish you'd earn enough Monday to Friday to hire a maid on Saturday so we could both enjoy our weekends."

Looking at Life
⚓ *MAY, 1982*

I have always believed that each and every one of us pays for what we receive. In short, nobody gets away scot-free and somewhere along the line there is a reckoning. I guess I believe simply that "there's no such thing as a free lunch."

As I grew older I began to question that belief. Dory and I had reached our mid-sixties and had our health, a modest income, and a wonderful way of life. Our two daughters were beautiful and seemingly content and happy. Our relationship with the kids was unbeatable. They were friends as well as children. We had found our version of paradise when we moved to Faro Blanco and it was made even better when our good friends Bill and Patsy Bolling tied up their yacht directly behind us.

In the spring of 1981 we realized a life-long dream of seeing Europe: after crossing the Atlantic on the *QE2*, we cruised the Canal du Midi in the south of France with our buddies, the Bollings; toured the French Riviera; visited Venice and Florence; spent ten days in Paris, and then flew home via British Airways. But within a few weeks after our return to Florida I found myself recovering from a serious operation and, while the prognosis was for a complete recovery, there were no guarantees that my disease might not appear again at some future time.

While the threat of another operation lurked in the backs of our minds, we figured such an unlikely event would be two or three years off. So, we planned a fantastic summer of 1982. It included another crossing on the *QE2* and cruises on both French and Dutch canals, in company with twenty-four couples drawn from my readers. Then Dory and I were scheduled to fly back to Newport for the *Motor Boating and Sailing* Trawler Rendezvous, followed by several weeks visiting friends in New England and New York before flying back to Amsterdam to cruise the Dutch canals on a brand-new trawler. Our next move would be to take the train to Nice where we had been offered the use of a bungalow overlooking the Mediterranean in Cap Ferrat. Then we planned to spend two weeks in Paris before returning to the United States aboard the *QE2*, our idea of a perfect way to top off a marvelous summer.

But this morning I found myself sitting on the bridge of *Simba*, looking at our beautiful marina and the surrounding waters, and asking myself, "Will I ever see Faro Blanco again, much less spend that marvelous summer we have planned? Will I ever spend another evening enjoying a cocktail and watching one of those spectacular Keys sunsets? Will I have the good fortune to have Dory kiss me goodnight and hear her whisper, 'I love you'? And will I see her pretty face when I open my eyes every morning?"

This was the last day of February and the next day we were flying to New York where I was to enter the Sloan-Kettering Institute for Cancer Research for an extensive rearrangement of my plumbing. About ten days ago I was given the news that the Fickle Finger of Fate decided it was time for another payment for all those marvelous years Dory and I had enjoyed.

I suppose we should have been in relatively good spirits. After all, I would be in the hands of the world's acknowledged experts in their chosen field. And, if the operation was a success, we'd be able to continue our lives pretty much as before. My surgeon in Marathon assured me that while I might have a few unusual accoutrements after the operation, I would be able to play polo, ski, tennis, jog, and swim long distances. I was quick to point out to him that I didn't do any of those things now and would prefer not to participate in them following the operation. You see, my idea of an active day is to have a heavy breakfast, sit at the typewriter for a few hours, then a light lunch on the bridge, followed by some more typing and then cocktails with Dory. Not what you'd call an active life.

As the time nears when we head off for Miami and the airport, I find myself looking around and saying, "Please let me return to paradise. Please let me enjoy the company of my good friends. Please let me walk down the dock holding Dory's hand. Please let my readers find their way down to the *Simba* and shake my hand. Give me another five years of status quo and we'll discuss the future at that time. Mind you, I'm not saying I'll be ready to go at the end of five years. But I might be a bit more amenable to the idea."

As you can see, I have no earth-shattering objectives I want to achieve. My life has been so rich, so filled with love, so packed with good friends, so satisfying, with so many wonderful memories and so many hearty laughs that the objectives set by most people seem a little silly to me.

Unlike most people, I don't want to live forever. I can't tell you exactly when I will want to depart this world but I can tell you the circumstances. I want to close my eyes for the last time exactly five seconds after my Dory leaves this world. I have picked five seconds because I think that is the maximum amount of time I could endure the pain of knowing she was not at my side as she has been these past forty-three years.

When summer rolls around I'll probably be living it up in Europe or gobbling that wonderful food on the *QE2*. And you will be saying to yourself, "What a sentimental slob that guy Bradley is."

Well, you'll be right. I am sentimental. It goes with being Irish. I'm not a bit ashamed. In a world run by computers and hard-eyed economists and power-mad presidents and worshipers of the bottom line, a little Irish sentiment might go a long way to reminding all of us that we were put on this earth to enjoy and to love one another and offer a helping hand to those in need.

And when they roll me down the aisle in Sloan-Kettering, I won't be ashamed if there are tears running down my cheeks because more than anything in the world at that moment I will be looking forward to seeing Dory's lovely face bent over mine, providing me with strength as she has for the past forty-three years. And if you can't understand that feeling, I have only pity for you.

My Kingdom for a Boat

⚓ *APRIL, 1978*

Of all the strange creatures God has wrought, the most unfathomable is not the eight-armed octopus, or the three-toed sloth, or even the one-armed bandit. It's the single-minded yachtsman.

Who but a yachtsman openly boasts of owning a hole in the water into which he pours money? Who but a yachtsman hangs on to his boat at his age when the cramped quarters, the swinging boom, and the hydraulic backstay threaten to do him in?

A tennis player will give up the game after a brief visit to his doctor. A golfer will sell his club membership on the advice of his accountant. A pilot will dispose of his plane at the mere hint of an IRS audit. But a yachtsman will borrow money against his life insurance, pawn his wife's wedding ring, and moonlight as a taxi driver to pay the taxes, storage, and maintenance on his boat. Once a man has blundered into the quicksand of yachting, he is a lost soul. Even as his head is sinking from view, his lips will form the words, "She's not for sale!"

Dr. Friedrich Ernst Seyfarth, dean of the Marine Biology Department at the Colorado School of Abnormal Behavior, has dedicated the major portion of his adult life to the study of yachtsmen and their quirks. Seyfarth believes a metamorphosis takes place when foot first meets deck.

"By the time a man reaches his fortieth birthday," says Seyfarth, "he knows he is not the master of his fate. What the federal government overlooks, the unions, women's libbers, and his offspring run. What does he do to escape? He pours himself a stiff drink, grabs a boating magazine, and locks himself in the den or the head. As he leafs through the pages, an image forms.

"He sees himself at the wheel of a yacht as it drives through cresting seas. His face is tanned and unwrinkled. His acne has cleared up. (Thank God! No more Clearasil!) He is bare to the waist and his abdomen is flat and well muscled. At his feet is a curvaceous young female, peeling grapes, which she places between his white, even rows of teeth. Before him in the cockpit are a collection of craven souls looking to him for salvation: his wife, his vile children, his IRS auditor, his mother-in-law. . . . Just as he starts to assure them that everything is under control, a voice calls out to him over furious pounding.

" 'Are you all right in there, George? You've been in the john for over an hour!'

"From this humble beginning many a yachtsman is born. Not long after, there comes the fateful boat purchase, and then old George begins changing. He develops a rolling gait, and switches from Chivas Regal to 'Mount Gay on the rocks.' At business meetings, he takes command when deadlocks are reached, and his boss marks him as an 'up-and-comer.' At home, his wife and children huddle at the foot of the dinner table and wait for his commands. George is transformed from a mouse to a lion. Suggesting that he sell his yacht is to suggest that he return to his former, ineffectual life. No, Mr. Bradley, once a man has tasted the glories of being a yachtsman, he will never return to his normal life. And now you'll have to excuse me. I must get back to my work."

He pressed a buzzer and his secretary, a forceful middle-aged woman with an aggressive air and the hint of a moustache, strode into the office carrying a handful of messages. As I walked to the door, I heard her tell the good doctor, "There's a call from the university president about your expense vouchers, two calls from that student committee on tenure, a note from your son about getting his allowance a month early, and a call about the IRS wanting to audit you next week. Oh, your wife is at the dress shop and said something about her account being overdrawn, and your mother has set fire to the rest home again, and . . . wait a minute! I'm not finished!"

The last I saw of the distinguished educator, he had a white admiral's cap on his head, a pipe stuck upside down in his mouth, a boating magazine in one hand, a pair of reading glasses in the other, and he was heading in the direction of a door marked "Men."

I'm not certain, but I think I detected a bit of a roll in his walk.

As the elevator doors closed, I thought I heard a muffled shout, "Hardalee! Trim your mains'l!" But it must have been my imagination. There are no yachtsmen in Colorado.

Are there?

The Out Islands, Chicago-Style

⚓ *DECEMBER, 1980*

What we don't know won't hurt us.

That's an outdated sentiment but there are times when I think it has a lot of merit. For example, a lot of fun went out of swimming after Peter Benchley published *Jaws*. A certain enjoyment of cruising remote waters was lost forever when Benchley wrote that ridiculous novel *The Island*. Son of Sam discouraged a lot of lovers from smooching in parked cars, the *Airport* movies convinced my wife she was not meant to fly and the *Towering Inferno* must have given a lot of New York office workers sleepless nights. I'd be happy if none of those books or movies had ever seen the light of day. But now something has happened that hits close to home.

A Chicago politician claims to have discovered a bullet-ridden and blood-spattered boat and a dead body in its dinghy while cruising in a remote area of the Bahamas' Out Islands. He was so shocked by this scene that he plans to take out full-page advertisements in the newspapers to warn prospective cruisers not to cruise or anchor alone in those waters. The legislator claims it was the work of drug smugglers, although how he comes to that conclusion is not known. I am particularly interested in this story because I was born and raised in Chicago and I love to cruise the Out Islands.

It's a known fact that a lot of drugs funnel through the Bahamas on their way to Florida. It's common knowledge that the Out Islands are infested with smugglers, and it is assumed that these fellows are not the type you would want to share a quiet anchorage with under any circumstances. Considering the number of couples who cruise the islands and the number of freaks there are in this crazy world, the chances were pretty good that some day a poor unfortunate couple would stumble into an anchorage frequented by some bad people and would suffer anything from robbery to death. I never forget that for a moment when I cruise the Bahamas. Or the Florida Keys or the Inland Waterway or Long Island Sound or the Chesapeake. I am also wary when I take a New York subway or a stroll after dark down the quiet streets of Newport, or Palm Beach.

What surprises me is the shock expressed by the Chicago politician over the discovery of violence. How could anyone live in Chicago for any length of time and not become accustomed to violence? I was born and raised in Chicago. I saw a man gunned down on a busy street at rush hour in Chicago, in a quiet family suburban area. I grew up reading about John Dillinger and the St. Valentine's Day Massacre and the mob. I can recall hearing a friend of my father tell about how Al Capone reduced competition in his market area by burying ambitious entrepreneurs in cement foundations. My memories of Chicago are so deeply etched that I ask for a bullet-proof vest if I fly over that town at thirty thousand feet.

I'm not advocating violence or a coarse attitude toward the people who apparently were murdered in that cruising paradise. I hate violence. I'm scared to death of smugglers, murderers, hijackers, muggers, dark alleys, dark streets, some streets in broad daylight, and I prefer to cruise in company and anchor with another boat. And if that other guy has an arsenal aboard and knows how to use it, so much the better. It's not that I'm scared. It's just that I don't want to have anything happen that will leave me scared for the rest of my life.

We lived in the Bahamas' Out Islands for one six-month period and have cruised the area frequently. Frankly, I have never felt safer in my life. So it bothers me when a man with access to some media makes a federal case out of a very unlikely incident and in so doing spoils what has been up to now a wonderful cruising ground. What was he expecting? Disneyland? A little slice of heaven? Adventure wrapped in a bullet-proof space capsule? The Bahamas are just fifty miles away from the most violent country in the world. Bimini is a short hop from the streets of Miami where the Colombian Cocaine Cowboys gun down people in supermarkets in midday. A murderer can push an innocent child in front of an oncoming train in the morning and be in Nassau that afternoon. Hotels in Nevada are blown up, volcanoes erupt, planes are hijacked, presidents are assassinated right here in the good old U.S. of A. Does that mean we should all hide under our beds? It's not a very nice world we live in these days.

The politician complained that it took the Bahamian police eighteen hours to reach the scene. Well, that's a long time, but then the

Bahamians are not as used to violence as we are, and when you're a hundred miles from Nassau you're a long way from anywhere. Which is why people go there in the first place.

I'm not saying the legislator from Chicago is all wrong. The incident affects each and every one of us who loves cruising the Bahamas. But to succumb to hysterics and condemn a government and advertise in newspapers to discourage people from visiting an area that depends almost entirely on tourism at a time when his own city has more crime in one day than the Bahamas have in ten years is unfair. I'm also not claiming that there isn't a lot of smuggling in the Out Islands. The papers report on it every day in Florida. I've always heard the Bahamians were tough on dope smugglers and were doing their best with limited resources.

If the good legislator wants to do something constructive rather than generate hysteria, he might urge our government to offer aid to the Bahamian government to fight the problem. And if we were more efficient at catching the smugglers when they reached our shores, they wouldn't be tempted to ply those beautiful waters. And if we could stop the stuff from ever leaving Colombia, those smugglers and murderers would just be a Colombian problem.

In the meantime, I intend to do as I have always done. I'll cruise in company of other boats, anchor with other boats, and hope that nothing happens to make me wish I'd stayed at home and missed all that beauty.

Publish or Flourish

⚓ *OCTOBER, 1980*

"For sale: one publisher's outfit consisting of tweed jacket, gray flannel trousers, suede vest, Oxford button-down shirt, knit tie, and suede cap, all purchased recently from Brooks Brothers. Size 42 regular. Also, one pair imported British shoes, size 9½, brown suede wing tips with crepe rubber sole. Like new. Worn infrequently over five-month period. Call Dick Bradley."

There, that should do it, I thought. A straightforward message that states the facts, no extra verbiage. All I had to do now was to place the ad in my local newspaper in Florida and wait for the calls to come in. After all, there are thousands of would-be publishers out there with great ideas for magazines the world should not be without. With luck I'd find someone who hadn't started his project and still had enough money to buy a new outfit. If he had started it, I knew I'd have to discuss terms with him. There is nothing that will part a man from his bankroll more quickly than becoming a publisher.

Last spring I came close to becoming a publisher myself. Never mind that a year ago I had trouble spelling publisher. All it takes is a backer with a lot of money, and supreme confidence in your own ability to know what the world needs in the way of a new magazine. Fledgling publishers never ask if the world *wants* the magazine they have in mind. It's enough that would-be publishers believe there is a *need*. And, for about five months, I was convinced the world really needed my brain child. Whether it did or didn't will never be known because the man with the money performed a financial hysterectomy on the project a few weeks before I began to suspect we were in for a miscarriage.

It all came about because I was trying to do a favor for a rich guy I'd sold a huge boat to some months before. He complained that his maintenance bills were too high, and besides, the Eastern Yachting Establishment hadn't welcomed him with open arms. I figured I was sort of responsible for his predicament. I'd sold him the yacht and made a nice chunk of change doing it. The least I could do was to see that he enjoyed it. That's the last time I'll worry about the happiness of a man who is said to have about forty million tucked away in the bank.

Anyway, I suggested that he buy a boating magazine so he could write off his boat expenses and, at the same time, be recognized as a patron of the magazine arts. He said, "Go! Buy me a magazine." But after trying for a couple of months to buy a boating magazine at a fair price it became obvious that the only solution to his problem was to start a new magazine. At this point I had my flash of genius and came up with the format for a very posh magazine for very posh yachtsmen. I gathered a group of experienced magazine people and off we tripped into the forest where the lions and tigers dwell. You see, we'd all done a bit of writing for magazines but we'd never really produced one. It was sort of an "Amateur Night at the Magazine Rack."

It was decided (mostly by me) that I would be publisher and Roger Vaughan, a terrific writer, would be editor. I then called my old friend Jock West, who used to be associate publisher of two boating magazines, and said, "I need advice. Can I hire you as a consultant?"

"Of course," he said. "Isn't that what friends are for? What do you need to know?"

"For one thing, what does a publisher do?" was my first question.

"That's an easy one," Jock replied. "A publisher worries. He worries about the size of the magazine and the amount of color pages and the cost of paper and printing and delivery dates and personnel and advertising pages and editors who tend to insult your biggest advertisers and dealing with the Mafia to get on the newsstands and making payrolls and keeping temperamental editors happy and . . . well, you get the idea. What else do you need to know?"

I thought for a minute and then asked, "Are there any good aspects of being a publisher? I mean, is it all bad?"

"No, not by a long shot," said Jock. "As a publisher you get to wear fancy clothes that make you look like you live in Darien, Connecticut, and you get to eat and drink in fancy restaurants on an expense account, and when people ask you what you do for a living you get to tell them you're a publisher, and you get to travel around to nice places and stay in nice hotels and circulate with interesting people who hope to sell you something so they treat you nicer than you're accustomed to being treated. Doesn't that sound like fun?"

"OK, that sounds good. But what do I do first?" I asked.

"First, you go to Brooks Brothers and let them outfit you in their Fairfield County Country Gentleman's Costume. Don't tell them you're starting up a new magazine or they'll make you pay cash. Let them think you're with *Fortune* or *Time*. Better yet, drop some book publisher's name like Harper and Row."

Off I went to New York and within a few days I looked exactly like a real live publisher. Except for one thing. My beard. Publishers are usually smooth-shaven with short hair. That's because they are basically either accountants or salesmen or both. Writers wear beards. The pressure to conform to the standard was severe. I withstood the pressure for several months, but I began weakening. I can recall standing in front of the mirror on several occasions, shears in hand, poised to start cutting off the beard I've worn for nearly twenty years. My wife screamed, "No! Don't do it. God only knows what you'll find under there. Wrinkles! Sags! Pimples, maybe! Let it be, even if you have to go on unemployment!"

Each time I'd cave in and simply trim it back a little, enough so you could see my tie and part of my shirt. Thank God I held off because the day came when two friendly looking barracudas walked into my office and invited Dory and me to have dinner with them at a swank restaurant. I remember it was shortly after we had downed a scrumptious meal and were starting on after-dinner drinks when I finally got around to asking them what they were selling.

"We're not selling," the younger of the two said. "I'm your money man's son and I'm here to tell you that we are canning the magazine project."

I looked at him aghast. "You can't do that," I cried. "I haven't had my compulsory heart attack yet. My ulcer isn't fully developed. I haven't even gotten my bill from Brooks Brothers."

I could tell by the hard look on his face that I was wasting my time arguing. I turned to the older fellow for support, but he'd fallen asleep. My whole life was flashing before my eyes, my career in publishing was ending, and all he could do was sleep!

Back to the young guy again. "What about the million bucks your dad committed to the project? We've only tossed a hundred grand down the drain. What about his promise to love, honor, and cherish our friendship until debt do us part?"

He looked at me and asked, "What's the matter? Can't you take a joke?"

"OK, then what about our friendship? How about when I sold him the big boat? And when we guided him around New England? And when I fired his captain? I thought he was my friend."

His face took on an icy expression. "That's the trouble with you poor people. You don't understand how the world works. You were never his friend. You were his yacht broker, his tour guide, and his hatchet man. What's that got to do with friendship?"

Come to think of it, he was right. Besides, if I'd kept up working like I was I'd have been dead in a month. So, it hasn't been all bad. But I did want to salvage one thing.

"OK, you win. But there's just one favor I have to ask."

He shook his head. "No, I won't buy your publisher's outfit. We have six of them in the storeroom now. You see, Dad tends to fly off on tangents like this every few months."

So, if you're about 5′ 11″, weigh about 185, and want to look like a publisher from Darien, I know where you can get a terrific buy in a like-new outfit.

It isn't that I don't like it. It's just that a heavy tweed jacket isn't worth a damn in Fort Lauderdale. And besides, they've never heard of Darien or Connecticut. Make me an offer.

The First Congressional Boat

⚓ *JULY, 1980*

Renowned historian Professor Petunia Goldfarb of Ingrate College has devoted the better part of the past decade looking for the answer to a question that has puzzled her colleagues for years: why did General Washington cross the Delaware River in the dead of winter instead of late summer? Recently, she turned up some notebooks that all but solve this perplexing mystery.

The discovery reveals a fascinating tale of delays and errors. According to the jottings of one Master Sergeant Ezekial S. Pimpernel, found stuffed in a small porcelain pot during the renovation of a home in Newport, Washington nearly went bonkers trying to organize his expedition to cross the Delaware and surprise the Hessians.

It turns out George's original plans called for a Labor Day offensive when it was assumed the Hessians would be laid back after a week of drilling and shooting stray members of the Continental Army. Washington had come across a Hessian directive that called for a week of raping and pillaging with a barbecue and bonfire to cap off the celebration. In what could have been the seminal "Abscam," Washington planned to allow huge quantities of potent rum to fall into the Hessians' hands just before the raid. Hessians had a reputation for loud snoring when sleeping under the influence of rum and the general figured this chorus would drown out the sounds of creaking oarlocks.

The plan was presented to the Continental Congress in April and

Government red tape kept George from crossing the Delaware
on time, while yard bills piled up.

was discussed for a few months before being passed on to the proper committee for action. Washington had requested 234 boats, with each vessel designed to hold 10 soldiers and an officer. This meant 5 benches crammed in the forward part of the boat and a lounge area and La-Z-Boy recliner in the aft section for the officers. (Life was not so democratic in Washington's army.) Congress, in its wisdom and true to form, had cut the appropriation, with recommendations that 20 men be packed into the same space and that a second La-Z-Boy recliner be installed for the use of a congressional observer.

The specifications were drawn up and turned over to the design firm Stevens, Chance and Peterson, thus assuring an eclectic approach to the project. Working drawings were to be delivered to the builder, a well-respected firm run by a woman, Minnie Ford, by May 15. But the postal service lost the first set in their newly installed package-sorting system and a further delay ensued while SC&P redrew the lines, this being before the day of the Xerox machine.

Meanwhile, a behind-the-scenes battle was being waged between the Ecology Freaks and the Government Department of Pragmatic Solutions. (This latter department has since been disbanded because of lack of funds and interest.) It seems the ecologists were against equipping the boats with buckets for relief, while the army insisted its men could not travel on water without such vital equipment. Additionally, there was a battle within a battle being waged as officers refused to share old oaken buckets with enlisted men, a tradition that probably exists today, the world being what it is.

A compromise was finally reached wherein officers would have buckets made of teak with holly inserts while enlisted men would get pine buckets with no inserts but the assurances of fully sanded rims. A note folded in the pages of Pimpernel's books talks of a bid by a firm called Ye Original Phybreglas Factory to supply buckets of a new material, but the offer was turned down as being "agin nature." No mention was made of the company's existence after this rejection, but it is my understanding a Delaware firm came upon the formula some years later and is still trying to perfect it.

Eventually, the plans arrived at Minnie Ford's boatyard and construction began. The first vessel off the assembly line had a peculiar chopped-off stern that one of the designers was confident would increase the apparent waterline while reducing the quarter wave or some such nonsense. Unfortunately, this theory was never fully tested because the boat sank immediately upon launching and drifted downstream with only the stern above water, its nameplate proudly displaying the word "Mariner."

Finally, the entire fleet of boats began to come off the line and they were then rowed, hauled, and carried to Washington's proposed launching site on the Delaware. By this time the whole affair had dragged on like the NBA season and just about everybody involved with the project had lost interest—except Washington, who had promised Martha a boat trip for her birthday, so he kept pushing for delivery. Finally, just a few days before Christmas, the last boat was delivered and plans were made to cross on the first clear night. The Continental Weather Bureau forecast a bright clear sky with a full moon on December 24. Well, as any of you who have seen that picture of Washington crossing the Delaware knows, it was a miserable night. It was so bad, in fact, that neither the congressional observers nor the officers showed up for the event, leaving poor George with the task of running the whole show.

The rest is history, of course, and inasmuch as I was never too good at history I'll leave it up to your memory or your imagination to fill in the story.

Needless to say, we ultimately won the war. Since then, not a hell of a lot has happened except that here we are in an election year wishing we had someone like good old George.

·SEVEN·

Cruising Without Cronkite

Down the Ditch

⚓ *DECEMBER, 1977*

"Don't you miss the change of seasons?" I'm often asked.

"Just as often as I can," is my usual reply.

This exchange generally takes place when the questioner discovers that my wife and I live aboard our forty-one-foot ketch year-round, spending our winters in Florida and summers in New England. The truth is, I hate cold weather. Just the thought of snow sends a chill up my spine. Standing too long before an open refrigerator door can send me to my bunk with a case of the miseries. In my world, ice is used solely to chill my drink. The thought of waking up to discover a film of ice on the decks can give me nightmares. Regardless of where I am, at the first sign of fall I up anchor and head South as fast as my slow boat will take me.

My wife, Dory, is a cold-weather person. She loves the sight of leaves turning. A brisk walk on an ice-encrusted beach in the dead of winter is her idea of fun. Sipping a hot-buttered rum in front of a roaring fireplace during a snowstorm is her idea of heaven. She fights leaving New England every fall until the last possible moment. The

193

closer we get to Florida, the glummer she becomes. Fact is, she doesn't get into the spirit of the thing until we drop the hook in some snug cove in the Exumas. Within two weeks of reaching the Bahamas, she's planning the trip North in the spring. Obviously, we have a problem.

Well, it could be a problem except for the Intracoastal Waterway. This is a series of canals, rivers, lakes, and sounds that wiggles its way from New England to Key West and allows us to make our 1,500-mile commute each spring and fall like a yo-yo on a long string. Zipping along at a steady 40 miles a day, we manage to complete a normal trip in about six weeks. This allows us to lay over in a few favorite harbors and do some sightseeing and shopping in cities like Annapolis, Charleston, and Savannah. It means we get an early start each morning and drop anchor or tie up in a marina by mid-afternoon, giving us time for a bit of reading and a nap before cocktail hour. On rare occasions we'll put in a 70-mile day to bypass an area we're not too fond of, and we've been known to cover 116 miles in one stretch. But we've found that hurrying defeats the purpose of the trip, so we dawdle.

What puzzles us is why so few couples make the trip. Even folks who have the time and money often hesitate because they've heard the Waterway is dangerous, boring, exhausting, and lonely. To which we say, "Baloney!" The Waterway is easy, safe, interesting, and filled with opportunities to meet a lot of nice people who are trying to get away from it all. Even the most inexperienced, incompetent, and timid of skippers can make the Waterway trip in total safety and peace of mind. Let me tell you about "Captain Heavy Weather and the Chicken Brigade."

The good captain owns a heavily built cruiser capable of surviving a trip over Niagara Falls with minimal damage, yet he never ventures out of the slip unless the skies are cloudless, the wind is calm, and the five-day forecast is for more of the same. He is the unofficial leader of a select group of timid souls who stay glued to the weather band of their VHF radio, hoping to hear something that will keep them tied to the dock for one more day. Each evening Captain Heavy Weather appears on the foredeck of his vessel and announces his intentions for the morrow. If he states his decision is to wait one more day, he is greeted with shrieks of joy and wild giggling. His followers prance up and down the docks, clinking glasses in toasts to their leader. Should he announce, however, that he plans to take off the next day despite a forecast of five-knot winds, straight down, he is met with silence and his band of chickens slink back to their boats to spend a worried night with little sleep. If I share a marina with Captain Heavy Weather and I see him untying dock lines in the early morning, I can rest assured there is perfect weather in sight. The problem with his program is it makes for a long trip and a short winter in Florida.

At the opposite end of the scale is the macho at the helm of a fast, wake-throwing sportfisherman who leaves in any kind of weather, puts 'er into full speed ahead and lets 'er rip until he roars into a marina some twelve hours later. This fellow leaves a trail of unhappy boat owners, landowners, and ecology-minded citizens behind him as he wends his way at high speed from marker to marker. The only time he lays over for a day is when he has his props replaced or his shafts straightened. When he reaches Miami Beach or Fort Lauderdale, worn out and a great deal poorer, he assures all within hearing distance that the "ditch" is a bore and he made it in six days this time. He often takes great pride in telling how many slower boats he rolled, how many people along the shore cursed him, and how he burned up umpteen hundred gallons of diesel on this trip.

We haven't found a solution to this poor sap. We've tried coming to a dead halt, dropping a "diver below" flag, and standing on the stern of our boat waving the culprit down. All to no avail. There is one popular brand of boat that we rate at 8.5 on the Richter scale. When one appears astern we batten down as though for a tidal wave and seek shelter up a side creek. What's really annoying is to have the skipper wave at you as you fight to control your boat when the five-foot swell hits you.

I used to get onto the VHF and comment on his ancestry, social standing, and IQ, but have recently switched to the universal sign language, which says it all without risking the loss of my radio license. Fortunately, not all big-power-boat skippers are this thoughtless. Most will slow down to a crawl to pass, providing you slow down to an even slower speed. I sometimes come to a total stop in the middle of the channel and give the onrushing offender a fierce stare. This is followed by either a smile of thanks or a raised fist with an up-pointing finger, depending on his passing manners. Why the hurry? If I was in a hurry, I'd fly.

Sure, there are a few minor irritants along the way. Take the flies in Georgia and South Carolina. These are the most vicious and annoying creatures I've yet to come across. They live in the marshes and attack passing boats like kamikaze pilots, zooming in at high speed and with little sense of direction. They are totally fearless and require repeated blows from an ordinary fly swatter just to get their attention. For the first few days I practiced my backhand but accomplished little more than to incense the little buggers. Finally, I switched to the Sunday edition of the *New York Times* and found that it required only two blows to do them in. The first dazed them enough to cause them to land and the second squashed them totally. Even then they kept swinging, much as I remember Jake La Motta back in the old days of the Saturday-night fights. Whatever you do, don't spray them. Most sprays act as an aphrodisiac to these flies, with you becoming their intended mate.

But an occasional rude skipper and a few battles with flies is a small price to pay for making one of the most beautiful passages a small boat can handle in comfort and safety. And what is more satisfying than knowing that while you bask in the sun, your friends and loved ones are freezing their fannies back home? As someone once said, "It isn't enough to win. A friend must lose." And the thrill that comes from dropping a picture postcard in the mail from Georgetown, Exumas, in February, to someone you love in Rochester is worth every penny the trip may have cost.

And speaking of friends, rest assured you won't miss your old ones, because they'll find you the moment you tie up in Florida. In fact, you'll be amazed at how many casual acquaintances suddenly turn out to be close buddies. You'll look up and there they come, the whole family—kids, pets, and bags galore—to spend a week with you on your boat. Relatives you've always disliked intensely will climb aboard, hard shoes glistening in the Florida sun, ready to drink your booze, and enjoy a harbor tour. Loneliness is not a problem once the word gets out that you're on your boat in Florida.

Your old friends will soon be replaced with new acquaintances who are making the trip at roughly your same speed. In fact, this is one of the real joys of the Waterway. The people who make this passage each year form a kind of floating, ever-changing community of dropouts. While they may range in age from the twenties to early seventies, they all share a love of boats, and most are enjoying the satisfaction of having turned their backs on the establishment way of life. By the end of the first week you'll have fallen in with folks who seem to be your kind of people. Cocktails on board somebody's boat after a day's run is what the Waterway is all about. After a while you find that your fellow travelers will drift away as you lay over to sight-see and they keep going. But then new boats will catch up with you and the scene is repeated over and over until you reach your permanent slip in Florida.

Ideally, you will find youself traveling with boats whose skippers have a huge tool inventory and who love to tinker with engines. If their wives are gourmet cooks and love to entertain, so much the better. We always look for overweight men with dirty fingernails and wives who look as though they spend their time slaving over a hot stove. The ultimate, of course, is to discover a couple with the above attributes plus a huge stock of fine wines and liquors.

I have one friend who is such a delightful dinner companion he seldom has to spend an evening alone, even though he has single-handed his motorsailer up and down the ditch for nearly twenty years. Jack Allen knows the Waterway like the back of his hand and loves every mile of it. According to Jack, his *Belinda* steers herself with only an occasional touch on the wheel because she senses when she is nearing a bank. Jack spends his time reading and soaking up the scenery slowly passing by. Should *Belinda* misbehave and run aground, Jack doesn't panic. He makes himself a soothing martini, goes back to reading his book, and awaits the arrival of a friend to tow him off the offending shoal. And, having made some forty trips, you can be sure it isn't long before he's back in the channel and on his way again. Not many of us know how to enjoy the Waterway as well as Jack Allen does, but we're learning.

Like most things in life, the unexpected comes along to throw your carefully planned schedule into a cocked hat. Take the Anti-Destination League, for example. This is a group of bridgetenders who seem to enjoy slowing down a boat-owner's trip by opening their bridges very slowly or not at all, depending on their frame of mind at the moment. I recall circling in a tight channel for an hour one night, blowing my horn at regular intervals, to no avail. Finally, the bridge opened and I was allowed to pass. As I went by the tender's shack I hollered, "Where in hell were you? I've been blowing my horn for an hour!"

I was put in my place by a lady tender who called back, "I was going to the toilet!" For an hour?

Another favorite ploy is to ignore your horn until you have been forced to make a U-turn and head away from the closed bridge. Just as you start back in the wrong direction the bridge opens, and you are forced to keep going away until you have room to maneuver. Finally, as you turn facing the bridge for your run, you note with horror that it is closing! This requires repeated horn blasts and some fancy footwork on your part to get through without losing your mast to the descending span. The worst of it is that you can't even complain for fear the tender will call the next bridge to warn that a troublemaker is on his way.

But these few soreheads are more than equaled by the good bridgetenders who open up without you having to signal. And as you pass through the open span, hearing the bells ring and waving to the people who've gotten out of their cars to wave wistfully in your direction, you have a feeling of power that's hard to equal. Occasionally, some spoilsport who's going to be late because of you manages to put a damper on the event. So I always keep a sharp eye out for a well-aimed tomato. So far, they've never hit us.

The point is, my friend, that if you have a boat and the time and a few bucks squirreled away, walk into your boss's office, punch him in the nose, and head south . . . fast. If you're not sure the boat can make it, just stay close to the bank so you can walk ashore in an emergency. If you perchance run aground, sit back and relax; some kind soul will soon come along and haul you off.

And if . . . excuse me a moment.

"What did you say, honey? The leaves are *what?* They're turning! Where are my charts? Where's my thermal underwear? Start the engine! Hoist the sails! Untie the dock lines!

"Kerchooo! Oh, God, I feel a cold cobbin on!"

Stocking Island, here I come.

Wine That Maketh Glad the Heart

⚓ *MAY, 1980*

Some people take all the fun out of life! Take wine experts, for example. They've probably done more to discourage wine drinking in this country than the Women's Christian Temperance Union. For some reason known only to themselves, wine drinking has become a science rather than a pleasure. This means that a midwestern, unsophisticated person like me is afraid to order a bottle of wine in a restaurant for fear of revealing his ignorance. As a result, I often find myself drinking light beer (which I hate) or Canadian club and water (which I love).

So, it was with a certain degree of interest that I read a wine column recently in the *New York Times*. The title of the column was "Wine Talk," straightforward and clearly understood. Here was a guide for the uninitiated wine drinker, I assumed. This was something I could cut out and keep in my billfold, to be furtively scrutinized when faced with an imperious waiter or a snobbish clerk in a liquor store. But the title of the column, unfortunately, was the only straightforward part of the article.

The opening sentence intrigued me, describing as it did a red wine of modest birth but regal bearing that had sold for $1.79 a bottle some fifteen years ago. Now, there was information that did me no earthly good. By now that wine would cost $23.00. I should have gone on to the crossword puzzle but decided I'd give the author one more chance. This proved to be a mistake.

You see, my knowledge of wine is confined to a few basic facts. It is either red or white and it comes in either a bottle or a glass. With that basic information I have managed to drink a fair amount of the stuff over the past twenty years. And, as my father used to say about whiskey, "Old wines are good, but some are better than others." Growing up on Chicago's South Side, as I did, left me with a suspicion that only sissies drank wine, except for the mobsters in Cicero who drank what was then called Dago Red. Fact is, if I hadn't gone on a diet I would probably not have taken much interest in wines and continued to gulp down whatever was put in front of me, along with large gobs of hot buttered bread and other morsels that delight the soul of a true gourmand.

But a skinny doctor had suggested that my problems with shortness of breath, inability to lace my shoes, dizziness when climbing stairs, and shirts with bursting seams all stemmed from a condition he succinctly described as obesity. That did it! I went on a strict diet, lost twenty-two pounds and developed a liking for wine's lower calorie content. I even began to like the taste! But I finally got a little embarrassed about ordering either a red or a white wine. Hence my interest in that newspaper column I mentioned in the beginning.

Now let me give you some examples of how a number of imported red wines were described by the expert.

Château Haut-Mazeris was "full-bodied and rich, with a chewy texture." For some reason I got an image of a wine-flavored wad of bubble gum and decided that wasn't for me.

Château Timberlay had a more pronounced bouquet but was less full-bodied and rich. This brought to mind a scrawny, impoverished woman who had lost her key to the shower room.

Clos Chantegrive was "austere," and conveyed a neutral quality that would be especially pleasing to consumers who prefer unassertive wines. I don't know about that one. I suppose it could be thought of as Casper Milquetoast-type wine, perhaps drunk by a third assistant teller in a stodgy midwestern bank. No, I think I'll pass on that one.

Château La Tour St. Bonnet "showed excellent texture and mouth-puckering astringency." That brought to mind a large bottle of unsweetened lemon juice. It also reminded me of the time my wife stored some Deks Olje teak finish in a wine decanter. My mouth puckered for three days after that one. I'll pass on the St. Bonnet.

Château Grand Mozerolles had an odd bouquet, a tannic taste, and a suggestion it might develop into something better over the next year or two. Sorry, I'm planning to start drinking in an hour.

Château Mont Belair was vegetable soup in the bouquet and taste and was very mediocre. Pass.

Well, I think you get the idea. What bothers me is that I've been sloshing down red wine without worrying about its "nose" or "chewiness" or "assertiveness." That makes me some sort of slob in the view of the wine freak. And to make matters worse, I've been known to drop a couple of ice cubes in my red wine to chill it! As for letting it "breathe" before pouring, forget it. The wine I buy comes out gasping for breath. One more hour and it would turn to pure vinegar. But what can you expect for $1.69 a bottle?

Having established myself as the quintessence of cultural decadence, I will now settle down with my jug of Gallo Hearty Burgundy, turn on my cheapo FM radio, pick up my current copy of *National Enquirer,* and enjoy an evening of gracious living.

Mother always said I'd come to no good end.

Father always used to say, "Get a job!"

My kids usually say, "Can I borrow a hundred?"

My banker usually says, "Are you kidding? How about the loan you already have?"

Dory says, "I love you just the way you are."

I always say, "Pass the cheese and crackers. And while you're up, pour me another red wine. Something textured, rich, chewy, fulsome, assertive, austere, astringent, tannic, and with a piquant bouquet."

Good Women Afloat

⚓ *AUGUST, 1979*

Most yachtsmen who live ashore envy me because I've lived aboard for ten years and have no plans to return to shoreside life. They complain that they'd do the same if it weren't for "the little woman" who hates boats, gets seasick at the sight of a dock, and has made it plain that if you want to go traipsing off on a boat you'd better get yourself a new wife. Most of these fellows don't have the sense to take that as an invitation too good to be refused. Sooner or later, they plaintively ask me how I manage this life.

The answer is simple: I made a good decision forty years ago and I'm enjoying the benefits today.

It's true. As of July 21, when Dory and I celebrated our fortieth wedding anniversary, I've enjoyed for four decades the benefits of having chosen the one woman in the world who could put up with me. It hasn't been easy for her. She once told a friend that living with me was like trying to run the 440 high hurdles with skis on. If she's been my anchor to windward, I've surely been her anchor to leeward. People who've come to know us can only shake their heads in wonderment. I'm as puzzled as they are, but I don't question my good fortune. I just enjoy it.

The whole trick to living aboard and liking it hinges on whom you share your life with. A mismatched couple who aren't happy on land sure as hell won't be happy living on a small boat.

Living aboard, to the average, mildly unhappy man, represents a form of escape. In his mind, a switch in life-styles offers him the opportunity to shed land-bound cares and worries. In his wife's eyes, giving up her precious furniture and possessions in favor of a cramped existence on a rolling chip of wood (or fiberglass) is nothing more than madness. They're both wrong, of course, because living aboard with the wrong person is no better—or worse—than living ashore with that same person.

In our case, moving from a comfortable house to a comfortable boat was not a traumatic occasion. Dory and I form a perfect union, and always have, but we didn't understand why until we moved aboard. While we are both Leos, we are totally different in our make-ups. Where she is energetic, I am lethargic. Where she is neat, I am sloppy. Where she is ambitious, I am lazy. Where she is organized, I create chaos. Without Dory, I would be a total disaster. I should feel sorry for her, but I don't because she knew what she was getting into before she married me. My father gave her the full lowdown.

My dad knew me pretty well. He used to tell friends, "Dick's butt will be glad when he's dead, because he's on it all the time." He also assured Dory she never had to worry about me chasing women because I was so lazy. What he didn't take into consideration was the energy of some desperate women. But through it all, Dory kept a firm hand on the helm and on me.

I think we would agree that the last ten years of our lives have been the happiest, perhaps because we have spent them aboard and come to really understand one another as we never did before. And to love one another as we never did before. We also appreciate how lucky we've been to find a life-style that fits us so well. Particularly at a time of life when other couples seem to drift apart, with the men spending their days at the country club and the women involved in shopping and gossiping.

Due to my improvidence, my days are spent at the typewriter here on the boat. I no longer disappear in the morning and reappear at night, totally bushed from having worked my butt off. Nor do I wonder what she does to occupy herself while I'm at the office. Dory's time is spent varnishing, painting, and doing the hundreds of other chores necessary to keep a yacht livable. When the day is done, we know and appreciate each other's contribution to the success of that day. Our lives are totally wrapped up in common problems and common solutions. Our days are full and our evenings are blessed periods of contentment. It's a good life, and I don't wonder that so many men envy my life-style.

But I assure anyone who says, "That guy Bradley sure leads a good life on his boat" that the secret is not the boat. It's the woman I married some forty years ago. Without her, the boat would be a shell. As would my life.

So, my advice to any man who looks forward to spending his golden years floating from dock to dock and anchorage to anchorage is simply to find himself a good woman. And then to hang on to her as if his life depended on it.

Because, believe me, it does. It really does.

Remembrance of Things Past

⚓ *JULY, 1981*

Do you occasionally find yourself reminiscing about the good old days? Or do you think that *these* are the good old days?

I got to thinking about the good times Dory and I had aboard an old fifty-foot sloop in the early sixties when she handed me her scrapbook. As I flipped the pages it brought back some great memories. Oddly enough, the warm feeling I have toward those days totally ignores the fact that I was collecting unemployment insurance, living in an oversized locker at the San Diego Yacht Club, and trying to keep my ancient Eight-Meter afloat while staying one step ahead of the bank and the sheriff.

When we bought that boat we didn't know zip about racing, but it was a low, lean and mean racing machine from Finland and it was built like a Stradivarius. *Cheerio* was about thirty years old when Dory and I acquired it with the help of the local pawn shop and a friendly banker. We got off to a slow start, and it was painful to know that the only thing standing in the way of victory was my total inadequacy as a sailor, much less a racing skipper. But I am part German and I stuck with it, reading everything I could find on the subject, and talking with experienced racing sailors like Lowell North, Jerry Driscoll, Ash Bown, and Malin Burnham.

Finally, by 1962 we were beginning to get the hang of it and our crew was learning the idiosyncrasies of the boat and the tide began to change in our favor. We still had a few hurdles to overcome that would have been insignificant if we'd had even a minimal income. Minor problems like winches that pulled up from the deck if too much pressure was applied, a fiber-glass spinnaker pole that bent like a piece of wet spaghetti, a shortage of winch handles, a very small inventory of sails (one main, one genoa, two spinnakers), no ship-to-shore, no RDF, no life craft, very few life jackets, an uncorrected compass, and a total lack of navigational equipment. Oh, I almost forgot. We had no engine. I'd removed it in hopes of rebuilding it and never got enough cash together to retrieve it from the rebuilder or get it put back in the boat. This meant we had to sail to the starting line and back to the slip. And as our racing record improved, the number of tows from friends diminished.

As I turned the pages of the scrapbook I came across clippings from the *San Diego Union* listing *Cheerio* as climbing up the ladder as the early weeks of 1962 went by. *Cheerio* was a light-weather miracle, a ghoster in light air. And San Diego is famous for light air. I had the right boat for the right place. The question was, would I learn how to sail *Cheerio* in time? The crew was motley to say the least: Herb Markowitz, a Navy captain and orthopedic surgeon; Dick Gant, now a successful attorney; Dougie Peterson, now a famous yacht designer, but then just a little kid who stole everybody's sweet rolls. And, of course, my wife, Dory, who never missed a race and who was in charge of "where is it?" and the galley and the running backstays.

My crew absolutely refused to race with me unless they were certain that Dory was aboard. There was some anxious moments, I can tell you, when Dory developed a cold late in the week and the whole crew would answer my pleas with, "Let's wait and see how Dory feels first." On overnight races her main duty was to hide the sweet rolls from Dougie Peterson and keep him from drawing pictures of boats on our bedraggled charts. I predicted he'd never amount to anything and, except for being a millionaire yacht designer, he hasn't. I am a shrewd judge of character.

We loved that boat. Not just Dory and me. The whole crew loved *Cheerio*, particularly when we were slipping through an entire fleet of racing boats in light winds. When the wind blew hard and our sails blew out and the sheets parted and the winches raised off the deck and we got lost in the fog with no radio gear, they swore at the boat but they were really swearing at the goofy owner who had the gall to try to race against millionaires with a thirty-year-old boat held together with string and determination.

Then came the 1962 Ensenada Race, with some three hundred fifty boats hoping for victory. All I was hoping for was to avoid a repeat performance of the last year's race and the one before that and. . . . But the Wind Gods were with us and it was a drifter almost from the start. If I recall we had either lost or forgotten our charts and my navigator simply pointed his finger in a southerly direction and said, "Go that way and follow the fleet." Not what you'd call an encouraging outlook on his part. *Cheerio* had one enduring quality. When the wind died and the rest of the fleet was doing 360s, she kept moving as though she had her own private breeze. And move she did, all night long, so that by daybreak we could see we were almost alone on a vast ocean.

I hugged the shoreline and got into what I am certain was a reverse current heading south, while the rest of the fleet was offshore fighting the prevailing north flowing current. Finally, a committee boat pulled alongside to tell us we were in third place, boat for boat, with the eighty-three-foot M-boat, *Sirius II*, and the sixty-seven-foot *Chubasco* ahead of us. We were in fast company! We crossed the finish line just behind them and closing fast. Then came a sixteen-hour wait while the rest of the fleet came in and the results were tabulated. Finally, a friend met me as we were coming back from a local bar, none the worse for wear, and told us we'd won the whole enchilada.

It was a thrilling time for all of us and Dory and I sometimes look back on those days as the best days of all. But I can't agree. It seems as though every year is a good year in retrospect. It's only the present that seems disappointing. And I am a perennial optimist who is certain greater glory and more fun are just around the next bend. But I have to admit the *Cheerio* days were marvelous and I have one very clear memory that I cannot recall or describe without getting choked up.

It happened as Dory and a crew member and I sailed back from Ensenada to the San Diego Yacht Club. It was dusk as we neared the club and started dropping sails for our approach to the slip. The wind was very light and as we drifted by the front porch of the club the voice of the manager came over the loudspeaker. Just a few simple words but words I'll never forget.

All he said was, "Welcome home, champ."

It still gives me goose bumps.

Confessions of a Continuous Convert

⚓ *MAY, 1977*

I'm as guilty as anyone on the water when it comes to looking down my nose at the other guy simply because he doesn't happen to share my enthusiasms at that moment. I'm talking about the caste system in boating that pits powerboatmen against sailors, sailing purists against everybody, and trawler owners against whichever side they decide they're *not* on.

I recall putting around Newport Harbor, California, in an ancient gas-powered, single-screw powerboat and wondering why anyone would work so hard to get someplace in a sailboat when powering was so much easier.

That was before I discovered sailing. When I did move from power into sail, I became the most dedicated convert in the land. Suddenly, I was a member of the elite. I joined a yacht club, became active in the social side of things, despised all powerboats, and avoided my former friends in power. When I looked back and saw a fifty-two-foot powerboat bearing down on me from astern, I felt hatred and panic as I hollered at my wife to hang on for dear life until "that S.O.B. in the powerboat gets by and things calm down."

It wasn't too long before I began racing and quickly discovered that the joy of racing depends on finishing in time to join the rest of the fleet at the club bar. Our boat consistently finished far back in the fleet and my wife finally said, "If you want to race, OK. But let's at least have a boat we can be sure will get us back for the festivities. It's either that or back to cruising." I immediately started a search for a fast boat, one that would make up for our lack of sailing and racing experience. I found it in a fifty-foot, eight-meter sloop named *Cheerio*, which had been built in Finland back in the late 1920s.

Cheerio had a sick engine and I prevailed on a couple of buddies to help me get it out and to a rebuilder. But by the time I was ready to install it in the boat, I had discovered the joys of sailing with no engine. So, I became the most obnoxious purist in southern California. I believed that anyone who had an engine in a sailboat was a traitor to the cause. I certainly didn't mind being towed to the starting line on a windless morning, but once the race started, I refused to acknowledge even a passing acquaintanceship with anyone whose boat had power.

Then came the day, after five years of racing, when it was time to sell the racing boat and go back to cruising. We got ourselves a forty-one-foot yawl with a reliable engine and over a period of a few years we slid from devoted sailors to part-time sailors to full-time motorsailors and finally to a trawler, the sailor's stinkpot.

After spending the summer of 1974 chasing the Twelves around Narragansett Bay, we decided we'd had enough of power and it was time to go back to sail. By the time we hit Annapolis, we'd found a buyer for our trawler and had acquired a forty-one-foot ketch. For two years we convinced ourselves we were having much more fun on the sailboat and wondered how we had ever managed to live without the peace and quiet of sailing. During this period we made it a point to give the trawler owner a cheery wave, just as though he was a fully fledged member of the human race.

Then came the fall of 1976 when midsummer skipped to midwinter overnight. We got as far as the Chesapeake by sail and made the balance of the trip south in a fifty-two-foot, twin-screw Huckins cruiser. By this time we were accustomed to being ignored by elitist sailors and semi-snubbed by trawlermen and welcomed by powerboat skippers. And it didn't take us long to find that we couldn't care less about who waved at whom just so long as we were warm and comfortable and making nineteen miles per hour toward the warm sun and water of Florida and the Bahamas. Each time we passed some poor half-frozen soul standing behind the wheel of a sailboat, wrapped up in mufflers, heavy mittens, and two suits of thermal underwear, we shook our heads and wondered what kind of masochist would subject himself to such torture simply to salve his ego. We had totally forgotten that exactly one year before, almost to the day, we had been in that guy's place, making fun of the powerboatmen hidden behind their oxygen tents and missing all that clean crisp air. Memory is short.

On the other hand, by the time we reached Florida we knew why powerboat skippers resented slower boats. Each time we slowed up for a trawler or sailboat, it meant coming down off plane, creeping along at a very uneconomical speed for a couple hundred yards, getting the boat back on plane, and then fiddling with the throttles for another ten minutes, trying to achieve a perfect synchronization of the twin engines. All of this time we knew the engines were gulping fuel and the boat was not running at its best. After a while, as we slowed to pass sailboats and gave the skipper a friendly wave, we found that very few acknowledged our waves or even expressed any gratitude for slowing down.

Also, we were amazed to find that many slower boats didn't try to cooperate with a passing boat. I frequently found myself slowing down to about 10 knots to avoid throwing a wake, but having a tough time passing a sailboat or trawler that was doing between 8½ and 9 knots. To get by, I had to increase my speed to where I was beginning to throw a wake; and I'd look back to see the slower boat rocking from side to side, the skipper shaking his fist. When we were in our sailboat or trawler we always throttled back to just above a dead stop to give the passing boat a chance to get by quickly and with no wake. The operator of the powerboat appreciated it and it was easier on us. But what can you do for a skipper who doesn't understand this simple maneuver? Not much unfortunately, and that's what produces hard feelings on both sides.

The whole problem could be solved if every boat owner was compelled to go through an indoctrination course before taking off in his own boat, whatever she might be. A month in sail with no engine, a month in sail with an auxiliary engine, a month in a slow trawler, and a month in a high-speed cruiser would qualify a boat owner to understand the other guy's problems and to do whatever is necessary to make it easy for both parties.

You fellows in slow boats should slow down to a crawl, tip your hat, and give a big smile as the faster boat passes you at a speed meant to reduce rolling to a minimum. Don't be unfriendly. Don't ignore him. He may pass you again tomorrow or the next day and you don't want him mad at you.

And you powerboat guys should remember that the man you're roaring up on is scared to death you're going to swamp him or send him careening up on a shoal. Slow down. Give the guy a chance to do the same. He can't help it if he likes slower boats. Forget the extra gallon or two of fuel you use in getting back on plane. It's peanuts compared to the total bill, and every time you're nice, you strike a blow for better understanding.

As for you trawler guys, I just don't know. You're in a never-never land. A trawler is like a sailboat without masts. Trawlers generally have round bottoms that cause them to rock unmercifully at the slightest provocation. Your best bet is to come to a dead stop and point your bow toward the oncoming wake. The skipper who's coming up on you will be so shocked he'll slow down to see if you're in trouble. At that moment, doff your cap, smile, and wave him on. Let him know you appreciate his efforts. It might start a whole new era of cooperation.

As long as you're on the water, whether it be in a canoe, inflatable, houseboat, sailboat, or luxury cruiser, it's all the same. We're all part of one big club and we'd best stop categorizing people as "purists," "blow boaters" or "stinkpotters." Every year sees more boats on the water. Every year sees our favorite cruising grounds becoming more crowded and slips harder to find. If we don't stop categorizing people, we're apt to have outright war, with everyone fighting for his own share and a little more. I hope that never comes.

Multihulls and Other Manias

⚓ *JULY, 1977*

It isn't easy working for a magazine that calls 'em the way it sees 'em.

Like, for instance, the other day a fellow sits down next to me at the marina coffee shop. I nod at him and go back to reading my newspaper. Then this fellow asks, "How come you guys don't like multihulls?"

I figure he's talking to someone else so I keep on reading. Then he nudges me and repeats the question. Well, I'm really not interested in talking to this character because he isn't your all-American, clean-cut sailing type. Behind a monstrous beard is a face that would make even the most loving mother shudder, and the way he asks the question reminds me of Peter Lorre in an old spy movie.

"Look, fella, if you're referring to *Motor Boating and Sailing*'s article about multihulls, you're talking to the wrong guy. I didn't write that piece and haven't even read it. So you're wasting your time picking an argument with me."

But that doesn't satisfy him. "How come you say you haven't read the story? Don't you read your own magazine?"

"No," I tell him. "I only read my own column. And I only do that to see if I can recognize anything I've written after the editor gets through rewriting it."

"Yeah, well, you guys said a lot of nasty things that we multihullers don't like. And we're looking to get even."

"Hey, buddy, get even somewhere else, will you? I got enough problems without having to defend my editor."

With this I get up and walk over to a table in the corner so I can continue stealing ideas from a Buchwald column I'm reading. But Old Multihull isn't satisfied. As he passes me on the way out he mutters something about getting even. I feel like telling him there's a long line of people I've offended in my articles who are waiting for a chance to get even. That's why I sleep with a shotgun next to my bunk.

I proceed to forget about this kook until a few days later when I notice that one of my dock lines has been cut almost all the way through. Then a couple of days after that somebody lifts my new hose and leaves a tired one in its place. The next night I hear two guys whispering outside my boat and I turn on the light just in time to keep them from climbing aboard. But I'm sure one of them was the trimaran nut.

I started spreading tacks around the deck but all that did was get me in Dutch with my wife. It seems she put the dog out to use the foredeck as a relief area and the first thing she knows the dog is howling with pain. She goes to the dog's rescue and suddenly she and the dog are doing a duet that wakes up the whole dock and brings the night watchman down brandishing a pistol. By the time I've apologized to everyone and begged my wife's forgiveness and bandaged the dog's paws and her feet, it's almost time to get up.

Finally, I write the editor and say, "Hey, pal, you may have got your jollies out of writing that put-down piece about multihulls, but my life is being made miserable by these guys. Can't you do something to get the pressure off? You know, sort of an apology or 'I was only kidding' kind of piece?" He suggests I write the story.

Well, I'm hardly the guy to do a story on multihulls inasmuch as I think that anybody who'd sail on a trimaran or a catamaran has a few marbles missing. About twenty years ago I got an idea in my head that I'd like to trade my fifty-foot sloop for a forty-two-foot catamaran. My wife and I went out for a trial sail and experienced the damnedest, most miserable motion we'd ever felt on a boat—or anywhere else, for that matter. After about half an hour of bouncing and jolting, I told the owner, "Get us back to the dock fast. This is the worst-riding boat or thing I've ever been on."

He agreed. "It's hell, ain't it?" he said. "Only used it one day and I've been trying to find a sucker ever since. Sorry you don't like it. But no hard feelings, eh?"

Soon as we got back to the club my wife and I rushed to the bar to fortify ourselves with a couple of milk punches. As we collapsed on the bar the bartender said, "Geez, you look beat. Like you was fresh off a trimaran."

"You're close," I said. "It was a catamaran. I feel like I'd just spent two days in one of those dodge 'em cars in an amusement park."

What I can't figure out is why people prefer one of those weird contraptions to a real, honest, single-hulled boat. A friend of mine has spent the last three years building a trimaran out of fiberglass. He and his whole family are pretty good-sized people and yet they've got a boat with a tiny cabin that will give them all the room and comfort of a telephone booth. I've never had the nerve to ask him why he made his decision because he's a huge bear of a man with a grip like a vise, and when he's had too much to drink, which is frequently, he tends to reduce strong men to a pulp by giving them friendly hugs.

Friends of his have warned me not to mention the boat to him, as it tends to make him violent. Seems like he spends a lot of time defending his choice of vessel. Sort of like Hudson owners used to back in the old days. They were considered the most loyal car owners in the country because they spent most of their time defending the car and their reasons for buying it. Unlike most multihull owners, this fellow is relatively normal. Except for those peculiarities I mentioned earlier.

The theory behind multihulls is that they're very light and will float *on* the water instead of *in* the water. This is good because you have to figure you'll spend a certain amount of your time upside down and it's comforting to know you aren't too apt to sink. Of course, the fact that all your food and possessions are floating around down below and all out of reach doesn't do much for your morale while you are waiting for a single-hulled rescue boat to come out and take you back to safety. Multihulls do not tow very well upside down, and therefore are seldom salvaged until they drift ashore on some island many thousands of miles away.

Your average boating person doesn't look on a multihull as the most seaworthy form of transportation. A woman I know recently got a letter from her daughter saying that she was on her way from Tahiti to Hawaii.

"By boat?" I asked the lady.

"No, she's on a trimaran," was the reply.

What could I say after I had reacted with a wince? I haven't anything against a trimaran, but as the man said—I wouldn't want my daughter to sail one.

Oldies but Goodies

⚓ *JUNE, 1979*

I came across an article the other day that claims it now takes about six thousand dollars to race a thirty-five-foot boat to Bermuda. Six thousand dollars! And that doesn't even include the twenty-four bags of sails and the monogrammed foul-weather gear. It wasn't too long ago that only a handful of wealthy men spent that kind of money on racing their boats. The rest of us got along with a lot less and did just fine, thank you. I know you'll find this hard to believe, but yacht racing used to be considered fun. You did your best to win, but if you lost, you either learned to sail faster or you learned to live with defeat. And the main reason for having a fast boat was to get back to the club bar in time for the party.

Out on the West Coast where I did my racing, the hottest "machine" used to be a twenty-year-old Owens cutter skippered by a wily fox named Ash Bown. Bown won races simply because he was the best offshore racing skipper around, and he knew his boat *Carousel* better than you know your wife. The last I heard, he had given up active racing, but still owned *Carousel.* How different from the modern racer who builds a boat for the Southern Ocean Racing Circuit, then sells it smack afterward for a profit or less, depending on how she finished in the standings. How in hell did the *sport* of yacht racing become the *business* of yacht racing?

It happened after 1962, which was the last year we campaigned our Eight-Meter *Cheerio.* Not having much of an income put a crimp in my ability to outfit the boat, but I managed by borrowing anything I could (sails, crew, beer) from boats that were not racing that day. My biggest fear was that the one and only winch handle would go over the side, so I tied it to the winch grinder's wrist. At least he was sure we'd come back for him if he fell overboard—something the rest of the crew couldn't count on.

I don't think I spent more than sixty-five dollars on racing that entire season. Each crew member brought his own food and beer, and nothing they wore was monogrammed with anything fancier than "Fruit of the Loom." To a man, they all were fearful that the mast would come down or the keel drop off our aging lady, and everyone wore foul-weather gear below because the decks leaked.

We dreaded a heavy-weather race with a lot of windward work because the genoa tracks lifted under pressure, the spinnaker pole bent alarmingly on a reach, and the mast looked like a piece of limp spaghetti in a rough sea. But the pole stayed together, the mast stayed up, and if the genoa track lifted too much, we tacked.

In spite of it all, we had fun. We even won races. In fact, in 1962 we won the Ensenada Race, with Jim Kilroy's *Kialoa* a distant thirtieth. Perhaps the shock of being beaten by the old *Cheerio* spurred him on to building a hot new racing machine the next year and starting a whole new era. All I know is that the old era was a good one. You couldn't buy a championship, there were more sailors than designers, and you could race and cruise to Catalina in the same boat. Good days.

Incidentally, there were over two hundred boats besides *Kialoa* in that 1962 Ensenada Race. But do you know who we were racing against? Just one boat. *Carousel.* And she came in second, less than five minutes behind us on corrected time. The thirty-three-year-old *Cheerio* beat the twenty-three-year-old *Carousel.*

I didn't think anything like that could happen again—until the 1977 Bermuda race. Won, if you recall, by a twenty-three-year-old Concordia yawl skippered by Arnie Gay, a sixty-year-old Annapolis yacht broker. A howl of protest went up from the also-rans in their almost-fast, slightly obsolete racing machines. There had to be something wrong, they insisted, when a wooden boat could beat a plastic one.

It never occurred to these skippers that Arnie is a fine sailor, and the Concordia is a fine design that lives up to the objectives of the rule to encourage wholesome, seaworthy boats. What really churned them up is that because of these two facts, nobody was hot to buy their IOR monstrosities—outside of a few aluminum collectors.

Arnie Gay told the Bermuda Race Committee that he was afraid he'd set yacht racing back thirty years.

I only wish he had.

A Tale of Two Women

⚓ *JUNE, 1977*

"Oh-oh, I think I just fell in love . . . again," said my cocktail-hour guest.

I looked over at my friend and followed his gaze up the mast of a sailboat in a nearby slip. My eyes came to rest on a husky-looking young woman perched at the masthead, working on the halyard sheaves.

"What's so great about her?" I asked. "I've seen better-looking girls right here on the docks every day."

"Yeah, I have too," he replied. "But they weren't on top of a mast fifty feet above the deck. That takes a special kind of woman. *My* kind of woman."

I had to admit he had something there. Most of the gals I've met around boats are reluctant to get close to a bosun's chair, much less allow themselves to be winched up a swaying mast. When my guest propped his feet up on the rail of my boat and took a long swig from his bottle of beer, I knew I was in for some homespun philosophy about women.

Sure enough, he started out with, "I've had a dream for over twenty years about finding the perfect boating woman. All I have to do is close my eyes and I can see her."

Naturally, I was curious to know what his dream girl looked like. Fishing a third cold beer out of the cooler for him, I urged him to describe the ideal mate for a boating man.

"Well, you understand that what looks good to me might not appeal to you. But my dream girl has to be a good looker because I don't cotton to ugly women. Then she's got a right nice build to her so's I'm happy to see her lolling around in a bikini. She's young enough to appeal to my baser side and old enough to know she's got a good thing with a character like me.

He described the ideal mate
for the boating man.

"When it comes to cooking, she's a gourmet chef and loves to act as bartender when friends stop over for drinks. Naturally, she's as neat as a pin.

"Like I always say, show me a boat without a woman and I'll show you a dirty boat.

"She's tops at celestial navigation, knows how to pilot a boat, understands engine repair, and fixes temperamental heads. Electrical problems are no mystery to her, and she can even straighten out basic electronic malfunctions. While I don't expect her to handle heavy construction, she's a master carpenter. She sews her own clothes, repairs torn sails, and is excellent at making one dollar do the work of three.

"Painting and varnishing would be her real forte, with spearfishing a sideline that keeps us in fresh fish year-round. She's fun to be with, bright as a button, and warm as a fur-lined parka. Her greatest pleasure would be keeping me supplied with cocktails and sandwiches and listening to my sea stories for hours on end. Her shoulders would be broad and her biceps well developed from raising the anchor and winching in the genny. She'd have an independent income and her folks would own a chain of liquor stores. Skinny-dipping and kissing would be her favorite pastimes. You know, she's just your ordinary all-American dream girl, yachting style."

With this he lapsed back into a semicoma, occasionally taking a pull of his beer. Then, suddenly, he jumped up and said, "I'd better get going. Here comes my crew."

I looked up and saw a rather nondescript gal of indeterminate age slouching down the dock. She obviously lived aboard a small boat. She had the hunched-over posture that comes from dodging a low boom, combined with the somewhat vacant expression that is the result of having ducked her head a moment late on one or too many occasions. One of her ears would be described by boxing fans as a "cauliflower." Her hair was sort of an alley-cat gray and was stuffed untidily into a worn and faded bandana. Her T-shirt was tattletale gray and wrinkled, as though it had just been retrieved from a ditty bag. She obviously was a member of the no-bra generation, but without the necessary credentials. Her perfume smelled like eau de bilge and her red hands had never been given the Oil of Olay treatment. There was black grease under the remains of her broken fingernails, burn spots on her arms from cooking bacon under way on a rough day, scars, cuts and bruises everywhere from a natural lack of grace, and her scrawny arms supported a huge bag of dirty laundry.

"Look at her," I said to my friend. "Somebody must have opened the sluice gate."

"Hey, man, that's my old lady!" was my buddy's reply.

"You gotta be kidding. What about all that 'dream girl' jazz you've been feeding me?"

He gave me a look over his sunglasses and said, "My daddy used to tell me, 'If you can't get five . . . take two.' "

"Well, it's obvious your dream girl doesn't exist," I told him.

"Oh, yes she does," he assured me. "Fact is, I found her once."

"So what happened?" I asked.

"Well, I tied up at the dock in Annapolis and walked to my favorite liquor store. Behind the counter was this gorgeous creature who turns out to be the owner's daughter. Man, she was something else. Well, I figured she had that outdoor look so I started talking about boats. Turns out she loves sailing and, yes, she'd love to go out for a moonlight sail that night. Luck was with me, and the moon was full and the air was warm and there was just a soft breeze. Right on time she comes walking down the dock, hops aboard, unties the lines, and fends off the pilings as we back out of the slip. Perfect, I tell myself, this gal knows how to handle herself on a boat.

"She gives me directions and in half an hour we're in a tiny cove that's just big enough for one boat. She drops the anchor and we snug it and while I'm securing the anchor line I hear a splash. On the deck I see a small pile of clothes and in the water I see what is obviously a girl. Well, it probably took me all of two seconds to get out of my duds and into the water. She pretended to be drowning and I showed her some of my more innovative rescue holds, including a few I extemporized for the occasion. Finally, we figured it was time to get back aboard and bone up on my mouth-to-mouth resuscitation techniques. This took about an hour before we had it down right.

"Then she excuses herself and slips down below to make us a couple of piña coladas. The moon cooperated at just the right moment and a lot of folks onshore probably got strained eyes that night trying to figure out what was going on. Next morning she has hot coffee and a great breakfast waiting for me when I get up. And the next thing I know she's sanding the brightwork. Boy, could she work. The only time she'd stop would be to go below and make me another drink. And every time she'd pass me she'd smother me with a long, drawn-out, steamy kiss. I can tell you, by the time we got back to the dock that night, I knew I'd found my dream girl. All I could think about was getting her before some other clown sneaked in ahead of me.

"So I put on a campaign to end all campaigns. Flowers, perfume, dinners, shows, gifts—you name it. Finally, I figured the time was right for making my pitch. I did a selling job like you never heard before. I'll never forget it. We were snuggled down in the cockpit of my boat, back in that same cozy cove, and everything was going right. Then I told her I'd been waiting for the perfect woman for twenty years and that she was it."

"So what happened? Did she say yes?"

"Not exactly. What she said was that she understood exactly how I felt. But there was just one hitch."

"Hitch? What hitch?" I wanted to know.

"Well, it seems she was looking for the perfect man."

Cruising Without Cronkite

⚓ JUNE, 1978

Like millions of Americans, I used to be a news junkie. My days were not complete unless I'd had my injection of the *Today* show in the morning, a complete reading of the *New York Times* with breakfast, *Time* magazine during lunch, an all-news radio station on my car radio, and two hours of local, regional, national and international television news each evening. The thought of being without the news while cruising the Bahamas sent a chill up my spine. Having to kick the habit cold turkey scared me to death.

The odd part of my addiction was that I really didn't give a damn about what was reported, nor did I remember much of it. It was a case of "garbage in, garbage out" and twenty seconds after ingesting a news item, it was forgotten. Like most newsaholics, I'd started out glancing through the morning newspaper and watching one of the major network news shows in the evening. But my appetite grew until much of my life was spent searching for the *New York Times,* adjusting the TV antenna, and fiddling with my radio dial in hopes of clear reception. My wife warned me I'd be mainlining if I wasn't careful but, like all addicts, I assured her I could kick the habit anytime. How wrong was I.

I recall the exact moment when I realized the full extent of my dependence on the news. We were in a beautiful anchorage on our first day in the Abacos, and I'd spent the afternoon working at the typewriter. My wife, Dory, came out of the galley and put a glass of Canadian Club and soda on my desk, a signal that my working day was over and it was officially cocktail hour aboard *Simba.* I picked up the glass and talked to the TV set, which I turned on. Then I settled down in my favorite chair and waited for the picture to come on.

"What are you expecting to happen?" It was Dory giving me a somewhat amused look. "Have you forgotten we're at anchor and about two hundred miles from the nearest TV station?"

Then it hit me. I recall breaking out in a cold sweat. My hands shook, nearly spilling my drink. There'd be no more television for months. No more cocktails with Walter Cronkite. No dinners with John Chancellor or Barbara Walters. No predictions of war in the Middle East, rising unemployment, inflation, strikes, murders, political chicanery, and international intrigue. No more traffic reports, inaccurate weather predictions, fatal accidents, and escaped hippos from the local zoo. New York could go broke and California slip into the sea and I'd be none the wiser. It was at that moment that I realized that Dory and I were going to be forced to revive an old and nearly forgotten social art . . . conversation.

As the weeks went by I found myself not really caring about what was happening outside the range of my VHF radio or my CB, the main means of communications in the Bahamas. Even though I could get Miami on my AM radio, the only station that came in clearly had both Paul Harvey and Ronald Reagan as commentators, a combination guaranteed to discourage much listening.

Outside of an early morning weather forecast sponsored by Charlie's Locker, most people stayed tuned to the CB radio. This was like a giant party line, with dozens of conversations going on simultaneously on the various channels. CB told you whether the Mackey seaplane was late again, who was having dinner at the Conch Inn that night, which of the bareboat charters was aground on what sand bar, when Jeff would have fresh eggs at the Harbor Store, if Estelle had baked coconut pies that morning, and countless other items of interest to all. If you tired of one conversation, you had only to switch channels for an exchange of gossip. It wasn't earth-shattering, but it was more relevant than either Cronkite or Chancellor.

Like most cruising people, I came to the conclusion that what we've been fed as news isn't news at all. It's nothing more than words the commentators have strung together and spoken in theatrical tones to keep us awake between commercials. CBS could televise year-old re-runs of Walter Cronkite and 90 percent of the audience wouldn't know the difference. In fact, not long ago I spent a whole day reading a copy of *Time*, and was shocked when my wife pointed out it was two years old. Nothing had changed to make me suspect it wasn't a current copy.

Somehow, and I don't think there's any one villain, we Americans have been brainwashed into believing that the political pirouettes of Sadat and Begin are more important than the need of the folks next door. The news media has given us a near-fatal overexposure to disasters, tragedies, problems, stupidities, and deceptions which do not touch our lives in any meaningful way. We have reacted by losing our trust in our fellow man, our concern for the problems of those who form a part of our daily lives, and our belief that the pursuit of happiness is not measured by how many cars we have in the garage at any one time.

Someday, perhaps in the near future, Walter Cronkite will sail his ketch *Wyntje* to the islands. I hope that he will drop anchor in the Abacos and decide, as I have, that paradise is made up of many small things . . . one of which is the absence of news that depresses me with its monotonous repetition of doom and gloom. I look forward to turning my CB radio on and hearing those mellifluous tones telling me about those vital happenings which relate directly to my life.

"Good evening! This is Walter Cronkite and the CB Evening News from Man-O'-War Cay. Nothing of significance to the Abacos has happened since yesterday. There were no tragedies, crimes of passion, robberies, swindles, cancer warnings, recalls of defective products, earthquakes, famines, plagues, political assassinations, or traffic pile-ups to report. The weather was gorgeous, as always, and promises to stay that way. The sound you hear in the background is that of a young bearded fellow playing his guitar in the cockpit of my boat plus the tinkling of ice as it is bathed in rum. And that's the way it is . . . and the way it should be."